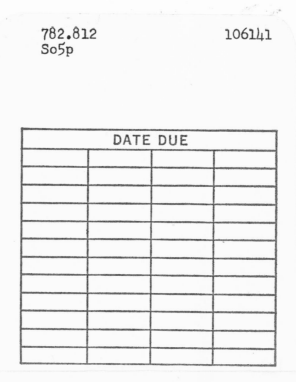

DATE DUE

PACIFIC OVERTURES

(CLOCKWISE) ISAO SATO, MAKO, SOON-TECK OH, CONRAD YAMA, FREDDY MAO, YUKI SHIMODA, SAB SHIMONO AND (CENTER) HARUKI FUJIMOTO IN "PACIFIC OVERTURES"

PACIFIC OVERTURES

Music and Lyrics by Stephen Sondheim

Book by John Weidman

❈

Additional Material by Hugh Wheeler

Originally Produced and Directed on Broadway

by Harold Prince

Illustrated with a drawing by Al Hirschfeld

and photographs

DODD, MEAD & COMPANY
NEW YORK

782.812

S O S p

1 0 6 1 4 1

Sept. 1978

Printed in the United States of America
1 2 3 4 5 6 7 8 9 10

Library of Congress Cataloging in Publication Data

Sondheim, Stephen.
   [Pacific overtures. Libretto. English]
   Pacific overtures.

   Musical play.
   1. Musical revues, comedies, etc.—Librettos.
I. Weidman, John, 1946-   Pacific overtures.
II. Title.
ML50.S705P3 1977   782'.8'1'2   76-55020
ISBN 0-396-07414-6

Pacific Overtures was first presented by Harold Prince in association with Ruth Mitchell at the Winter Garden Theatre, New York City, on January 11, 1976.

NOTE

Pacific Overtures borrows liberally from the techniques of the Japanese *kabuki* theater in every aspect of its production and performance. Freely adapted for use on the American musical stage, these techniques include the playing of women's roles by men; the use of a *Reciter*, who alternately comments on the action, joins it, or speaks in place of one of the other characters; the presence of a *hanamichi*, or runway, which allows performers to make entrances and exits through the house; and the changing of props and costumes onstage by a group of stagehands clad in black. Black being the color of non-existence, these stagehands are literally invisible as far as a Japanese audience is concerned.

CAST

Reciter	Mako
Abe, First Councilor	Yuki Shimoda
Manjiro	Sab Shimono
Second Councilor	James Dybas
Shogun's Mother	Alvin Ing
Third Councilor	Freddy Mao
Kayama	Isao Sato
Tamate (Kayama's Wife) *Samurai* *Storyteller* *Swordsman*	Soon-Teck Oh
Samurai	Ernest Abuba, Mark Hsu Syers
Servant	Haruki Fujimoto
Observers	Alvin Ing, Ricardo Tobia
Fisherman	Jae Woo Lee
Merchant	Alvin Ing
Son	Timm Fujii
Grandmother	Conrad Yama
Thief	Mark Hsu Syers
Adams	Ernest Abuba
Williams	Larry Hama
Commodore Matthew Calbraith Perry	Haruki Fujimoto
Shogun's Wife	Freda Foh Shen
Physician	Ernest Harada

Priests	Timm Fujii, Gedde Watanabe
Soothsayer	Mark Hsu Syers
Sumo Wrestlers	Conrad Yama, Jae Woo Lee
Shogun's Companion	Patrick Kinser-Lau
Shogun	Mako
Madam	Ernest Harada
Girls	Timm Fujii, Patrick Kinser-Lau, Gedde Watanabe, Leslie Watanabe
Old Man	James Dybas
Boy	Gedde Watanabe
Warrior	Mark Hsu Syers
Imperial Priest	Tom Matsusaka
Nobles	Ernest Abuba, Tim Fujii
American Admiral	Alvin Ing
British Admiral	Ernest Harada
Dutch Admiral	Patrick Kinser-Lau
Russian Admiral	Mark Hsu Syers
French Admiral	James Dybas
Lords of the South	Larry Hama, Jae Woo Lee
Jonathan Goble	Mako
Japanese Merchant	Conrad Yama
Samurai's Daughter	Freddy Mao
British Sailors	Timm Fujii, Patrick Kinser-Lau, Mark Hsu Syers
Musician	Joey Ginza

Proscenium Servants, Sailors and Townspeople
Susan Kikuchi, Diane Lam, Kim Miyori, Freda Foh Shen, Kenneth S. Eiland, Timm Fujii, Joey Ginza, Patrick Kinser-Lau, Tony Marinyo, Kevin Maung, Dingo Secretario, Mark Hsu Syers, Ricardo Tobia, Gedde Watanabe, Leslie Watanabe

Musicians	Fusako Yoshida (Shamisen), Genji Ito (Percussion)

ACT I

Scene 1

THREE JAPANESE MUSICIANS *enter and take positions on a low platform at the side of the stage. One plays briefly on the shamisen and sings. From Offstage comes the sound of a bass drum beaten furiously and then wooden blocks sharply striking the floor.*

The stage and the auditorium go to black.

The stage and house lights bump up revealing the RECITER *in front of the show curtain, forehead touching the floor in prayer. The blocks are struck again.*

RECITER   Nippon. The Floating Kingdom. An island empire which for centuries has lived in perfect peace, undisturbed by intruders from across the sea. There was a time when foreigners were welcome here, but they took advantage of our friendship. Two hundred and fifty years ago we drove them out—by sacred decree of the great Shogun Tokugawa —and ordered them never again to set foot on our ancestral soil. From then until this day, in the month of July, 1853, there has been nothing to threaten the serene and change-less cycle of our days.

(A STAGEHAND *runs the show curtain across the stage, revealing the* MEMBERS OF THE COMPANY. *They are a cross-section of mid-nineteenth-century Japanese society, everything from farmers to samurai.*)

In the middle of the world we float
In the middle of the sea.
The realities remain remote
In the middle of the sea.
Kings are burning somewhere,
Wheels are turning somewhere,
Trains are being run,
Wars are being won,
Things are being done
Somewhere out there, not here.
Here we paint screens.
Yes . . . the arrangement of the screens:

We sit inside the screens
And contemplate the view
That's painted on the screens
More beautiful than true.
Beyond the screens
That glide aside
Are further screens
That open wide
With scenes of screens like the ones that glide.
And no one presses in,
And no one glances out,
And kings are burning somewhere,

ALL   Not here!

As the hurricanes have come, they've passed
In the middle of the sea.
The advantages are made to last
In the middle of the sea.
Gods are crumbling somewhere,
Machines are rumbling somewhere,

Ways are being found,
Watches being wound,
Prophets being crowned
Somewhere out there, not here.
Here we plant rice.

RECITER   Yes. The arrangement of the rice:

    (*The* COMPANY *demonstrates*)

The farmer plants the rice.
The priest exalts the rice.
The Lord collects the rice.
The merchant buys the rice.
The craftsman makes the sword
And sells it to the lord
And buys at twice the former price
What he counts on his lord to protect with his sword:

ALL   The rice.

RECITER

They eat the rice and then
The day begins again,

ALL

And gods are crumbling somewhere—
Not here!

The disturbances are worlds away
In the middle of the sea.
And tomorrow will be like today
In the middle of the sea.
Blood is flowing somewhere,
Ideas are growing somewhere,
Trails are being blazed,

Voices being raised,
Women being praised
Somewhere out there, not here.
Here we trade bows.

RECITER   Yes. The arrangement of the bows:

> (TWO STAGEHANDS *enter carrying a tiny puppet dressed in regal robes.* EVERYONE *immediately drops to the ground, forehead down*)

First for the Emperor,
Descendant of the sun-goddess Amaterasu!
All-knowing and all-powerful!
Ruler absolute!
One year old.

> (*As the puppet*/EMPEROR *is carried off,* TWO BEARERS *enter and cross the stage carrying a curtained palanquin*)

Second for the Shogun,
Protector of the kingdom,
Keeper of the peace.
Seldom seen.

> (*As the* BEARERS *exit,* TWO FEUDAL LORDS *swagger on*)

Then for the Lords of the South,
Vassals to the Shogun,
Loyal to their master . . .
Not for long.

> (*The* TWO LORDS *exit as* EVERYONE *stands*)

And kings are burning somewhere,

ALL   Not here!

The advantages go on and on
In the middle of the sea.
As the centuries have come, they've gone
In the middle of the sea.
Days arise to be replaced,
Lines are drawn and lines erased.
Life and death are but verses in a poem.
Out there blood flows.
Who knows?
Here we paint screens,

GROUP A

Plant the rice,

GROUP B

Arrange the flowers,

GROUP A

View the moon,

GROUP B

Exchange the gifts,

GROUP A

Plant the rice,

ALL

Arrange tomorrow like today to float,
Slide the screens,
Exchange the poems,
Stir the tea,
Exchange the bows,
Plant the rice,
Arrange tomorrow to be like today,
To float.

GROUP A	GROUP B
The viewing of the moon,	The viewing of the moon,
The planting of the rice,	The planting of the rice,
The stirring of the tea,	The stirring of the tea,
The painting of the screens.	The painting of the screens.
	We float.
The viewing of the moon,	
	The stirring of the tea,
The planting of the rice,	The folding of the fans.
The weaving of the mats.	We float.
	The placing of the stones,
We float.	The painting of the sliding screens,
The viewing of the moon,	The wrapping of the gifts,
The planting of the rice,	The sliding of the painted screens.
	We float.
The catching of the fish,	The weaving of the mats,
	The stirring of the tea,
The painting of ...	We float ...
We float ...	

(*The* LAST MEMBER OF THE COMPANY *exits, leaving the* RECITER *alone on stage*)

RECITER   We float.

(*Speaks*)

Even in a land of changeless order, there are sometimes slight—disturbances. Nothing of importance, nothing threatening or distressing. A piece of gossip from a noodle seller, or the languorous whisper of a geisha. "I hear ... I heard ... The rice merchant is sure ..." Just a rumor, to be noted —and dismissed. Nothing of importance, nothing—but wait, there is another one! "Who? . . . And where? . . . You say you saw the cage yourself?"

(A PROCESSION *down the hanamichi:* TWO BEARERS *carrying a cage/palanquin, in which a* JAPANESE *in Western sailor's dress sits crouched*)

A prisoner in Western dress, conveyed to Edo in the dead of night. There to be examined by the mighty Shogun himself, surrogate to an emperor far too holy to be sullied by mortal eyes. The Shogun!

(A *curtain drops, revealing the* SHOGUN'*s court. Present are* LORD ABE, *First Councilor to the* SHOGUN, *the* SECOND *and* THIRD COUNCILORS *to the* SHOGUN, *and the* SHOGUN'*s* MOTHER. *The* SHOGUN *is absent*)

Oh dear, no Shogun. Perhaps his stars today are inauspicious for an audience.

(*The* BEARERS *carry the cage/palanquin into the court and put it down*)

ABE   The prisoner's name?

THIRD COUNCILOR   John Manjiro, my lord.

ABE   Where does he come from?

RECITER   The questioner is Lord Abe, representing the Shogun in his absence.

THIRD COUNCILOR   Nakahama, lord. A fishing village on the south coast of Shikoku.

ABE   And do all the residents of Nakahama wear such foreign dress?

THIRD COUNCILOR   No, my lord.

ABE   Then you will explain his appearance.

THIRD COUNCILOR (*Reading from a scroll*)   He is a fisherman, my lord. Six years ago his boat was driven out to sea by storms. He was rescued by the captain of a barbarian ship, who took him to a place called Massachusetts, where he went to school. From there—

MOTHER (*Interrupting*)   What does this mean?

RECITER   The Shogun's mother.

THIRD COUNCILOR   That he has come here from America.

MOTHER   America?

SECOND COUNCILOR   But why has he come back? Does he not know that he has violated our laws twice—first when he left Japan, and then when he returned? Each crime is punishable by death.

(*To* MANJIRO)

Why have you come back?

RECITER (*Speaking for* MANJIRO)   There were rumors in America, my lord. Rumors which I thought my countrymen should hear.

SECOND COUNCILOR   What did the rumors say?

RECITER (*For* MANJIRO)   That America would send an expedition to Japan.

ABE (*Carefully*)   And are these rumors true?

RECITER (*For* MANJIRO)   They are, my lord. As I made my way back home I stopped in Okinawa. In the harbor there were four black ships, Western warships, fitted out with giant cannon, manned by sailors, armed with weapons such as you have never seen. Americans, my lord, and their ships are coming here!

THIRD COUNCILOR   It is obvious. The man is a traitor, sent here by the Westerners to spy on us.

RECITER (*For* MANJIRO)   My lord, I'm not! I swear to you! Even as we speak the ships are on their way. You must prepare yourselves to deal with them. You must—

THIRD COUNCILOR (*Interrupting*)   You dare to tell Lord Abe what to do!

RECITER (*For* MANJIRO)   My lord, I—

THIRD COUNCILOR   You dare suggest that we meet face to face with Western dogs!

SECOND COUNCILOR   That we subject ourselves to such humiliation!

ABE   If he saw the ships at Okinawa, they will be here—any day.

(ABE *gestures and the* BEARERS *exit with* MANJIRO's *cage*)

When the Americans arrive, someone will have to deal with them. Someone, but who?

(*On another playing area, a young* SAMURAI *enters, followed by his* WIFE)

RECITER   Kayama Yesaemon. A samurai, but one of little consequence. He and his wife Tamate have been fishing. This year they cast their nets in streams belonging to the Shogun. A transgression to be sure, but one well worth the risk, for they have caught the lucky ayu, a fish which portends one year of good fortune.

(*Two* SAMURAI *appear and block* KAYAMA'*s path*)

FIRST SAMURAI   Kayama Yesaemon?

(KAYAMA *nods*)

SECOND SAMURAI   You are wanted by the Shogun's Councilors.

FIRST SAMURAI   You are to come with us at once.

KAYAMA   But why? I—

SECOND SAMURAI (*Interrupting*)   It is not your business to ask why.

(KAYAMA *bows and turns to* TAMATE)

KAYAMA   Wait for me, Tamate. Wait at home.

TAMATE (*Urgently*)   Tell them that we meant no harm. Tell them—

KAYAMA (*Interrupting*)   Wait for me at home.

(TAMATE *exits as* KAYAMA *turns and steps from his playing area into the* SHOGUN'S *court. He prostrates himself before* LORD ABE)

ABE   Kayama Yesaemon?

KAYAMA   Yes, my lord.

ABE   Your rank?

KAYAMA   Secretary to the Governor of Uraga. And if in some way I have offended—

SECOND COUNCILOR   Silence!

THIRD COUNCILOR   Hold your tongue!

KAYAMA (*Humiliated*)   Yes, my lord.

ABE   From today you have become Prefect of Police for the entire city of Uraga.

KAYAMA   I—I have? My lord, I humbly thank you for this great honor and will do all in my power to be worthy of your trust!

ABE   Yes—you will!

RECITER   A haiku: A gift unearned
                    And unexpected
                    Often has a hidden price.

ABE   And so, when the Americans arrive, you will take a boat to their ships and you will order them to return immediately from whence they came. Is that understood?

KAYAMA   I . . . my lord . . . in a boat, my lord . . . ordering . . . ?

ABE   You will inform them of the sacred decree. You will terrify them with the fate that awaits all foreign devils who dare to set foot on our holy soil. Kayama Yesaemon, may the Gods of our fathers make you equal to this awesome task!

ACT I

Scene 2

A small Japanese house is revealed Upstage. The COURT *exits.* KAYAMA *walks into the house, where he is joined by* TAMATE.

TAMATE   What did the Councilors say?

KAYAMA   They have appointed me Prefect of Police of the city of Uraga.

TAMATE   But, this is wonderful, to receive such happy news when we expected—

KAYAMA (*Interrupting*)   It is not happy news, Tamate. There are foreign warships on their way to Japan. They will first be sighted off Uraga, and it will be the duty of the Prefect of Police to go out to meet them—and drive them away.

TAMATE   But how—if they are so powerful?

KAYAMA   I do not know.

TAMATE   And if they refuse to go . . . ?

KAYAMA   It will be a great disgrace, so great that no one near the Shogun's throne would dare to deal with these barbarians. That is the only reason why I have been chosen.

TAMATE (*Pause*)   Perhaps the foreigners will not come.

KAYAMA   They will come. And should I fail, you know what we must do.

(KAYAMA *begins to remove his short sword from its
sheath and* TAMATE *starts up in alarm. Suddenly a bell
sounds in the distance*)

The Americans are here!

(*A shakuhachi plays a mournful solo.* TWO OBSERVERS
appear. TAMATE *dances as the* OBSERVERS *sing. The*
FIRST *sings about her, the* SECOND *sings her words and
thoughts*)

FIRST OBSERVER
The eye sees, the thought flies.
The eye tells, the thought denies.

SECOND OBSERVER
I will prepare for your returning.
(Is there no other way?)

FIRST OBSERVER
The word falls, the heart cries.
The heart knows the word's disguise.

SECOND OBSERVER
I shall expect you then at evening.
(Is there no other way?)

FIRST OBSERVER
The bird sings, the wind sighs,
The air stirs, the bird shies.
A storm approaches.

SECOND OBSERVER
(There must be other ways . . .)

FIRST OBSERVER
The leaf shakes, the wings rise.

The song stops, the bird flies.
The storm approaches.

SECOND OBSERVER
I will have supper waiting.

FIRST OBSERVER
The song stops, the bird flies.
The mind stirs, the heart replies,
"There is no other way."

SECOND OBSERVER
I shall expect you then at evening.

(*The bell sounds again.* TAMATE *pauses before* KAYAMA.
He hesitates, then turns quickly on his heel and exits)

FIRST OBSERVER
The word stops, the heart dies.
The wind counts the lost goodbyes.

SECOND OBSERVER
There is no other way.
There is no other way.

(TAMATE *takes a sheathed knife from the household
shrine, kneels, pulls the knife halfway out, then looks
up sharply as the bell sounds once again*)

ACT I

Scene 3

An enormous bell is lowered from the flies, and a FISH-
ERMAN *rushes on and pumps it wildly.*

FISHERMAN (*Sings*)
  I was standing on the beach
  Near the cliffs
  At Oshima.
  I was spreading out the nets
  For the morning sun.
  It was early in July
  And the day was getting hot,
  And I stopped to wipe my eyes,
  And by accident I turned
  And looked out to sea . . .

  And there came,
  Breaking through the mist,
  Roaring through the sea,
  Four black dragons,
  Spitting fire.
  And I ran,
  Cursing through the fields,
  Calling the alarm,
  Shouting to the world,
  "Four black dragons!
  Spitting fire!"

And the earth trembled,
And the sky cracked,
And I thought it was the end of the world.

(*A* MERCHANT *and his* FAMILY *enter. The* FISHERMAN
returns to the bell. The MERCHANT *leads a horse, which
is loaded down with sacks and boxes. The* MERCHANT'S
SON *also carries a number of bundles, and in his haste
he trips and drops them*)

MERCHANT   Pick them up, you clumsy oaf! No, wait. Come
take these instead.

(*He hands his* SON *several lacquer boxes*)

And hurry! If we are not out of here before the barbarians
come, they will kill us all.

SON (*Trying to tie the boxes on the horse*)   The horse is
loaded, father. There is room for nothing else.

MERCHANT   What? Leave my fortune here to be destroyed by
foreign dogs! I'll stay and fight before—

(*He is interrupted by underscoring, indicating the ap-
proaching invaders*)

God save us! Grab the horse's reins. No, get your grandmother. There is no time to lose. All right then. Everybody
ready?

(*The* GRANDMOTHER *doesn't move*)

GRANDMOTHER   A mother does not walk. She rides.

MERCHANT   What!

GRANDMOTHER   A mother does not walk. She rides.

MERCHANT   But the horse's legs are buckling as it is.

GRANDMOTHER   A mother does not—

MERCHANT (*Interrupting*)   All right, all right!

(*Gesturing to his* SON)

Here, push those sacks aside.

(*They try to hoist the* GRANDMOTHER *up on the horse, but it trembles under the weight, then drops down to its knees*)

You see? You will have to walk with the rest of us.

GRANDMOTHER   I would rather stay behind and be ravished by the barbarians.

MERCHANT (*Exasperated*)   As you wish. Come on then! Come!

(*The* FAMILY *turns to go*)

RECITER   Confucius tells the story of a merchant who grew tired of caring for his aged mother. He called his son and told him to prepare a litter, so that they might carry the feeble old woman out to the countryside to die. The young boy set to work, and when the man returned, he found his son had built, not one litter, but two. "The first one is the one you asked for," explained the boy, "and the second I shall save and use when you have grown as old as grandmother."

MERCHANT   Oh, all right! Come on then!

(*He throws his* MOTHER *on his back and the* ENTIRE FAMILY *rushes off pell mell*)

Come!

(A THIEF *enters as they leave*)

THIEF (*Sings*)
I was rifling through the house
Of some priests
In Uraga.
It was only after dawn,
They were sleeping still.
I had finished with the silks,
I was hunting for the gold,
When I heard them getting up,
So I bolted through a door . . .
Which looked out to sea . . .

FISHERMAN
And there came . . .

THIEF
And there came . . .

FISHERMAN
Breaking through the mist . . .

THIEF
Boiling through the mist . . .

FISHERMAN
Roaring through the sea . . .

THIEF
Rising from the sea . . .

FISHERMAN
Four black dragons . . .

THIEF
Four volcanoes . . .

FISHERMAN
   Spitting fire . . .

THIEF
   Spitting fire!
   And I ran . . .

FISHERMAN
   And I ran . . .

THIEF
   Cursing down the halls . . .

FISHERMAN
   Cursing through the fields . . .

THIEF
   Shouting to the priests . . .

FISHERMAN
   Shouting to the world . . .

BOTH
   "Notify the gods!

THIEF	FISHERMAN
Four volcanoes,	Four black dragons,
Spitting fire!"	Spitting fire!"

RECITER (*Sings, very quietly*)
   And the feet pattered
   As the men came down to stare,
   And the women started screaming
   Like the gulls.
   Hai!
   Hai!

(Each time the RECITER *gives his small scream,* TOWNS-
PEOPLE *appear, delicately showing alarm. They stare,
point, and as the panic grows, run bewilderedly. The
effect should be one of a Japanese watercolor riot)*

And they crowded into temples
And they flapped about the square—
Hai!—
Like the gulls.
Hai!

TOWNSPEOPLE

Hai! Hai!
Four black dragons,
Spitting fire!

RECITER

Then the hooves clattered
And the warriors were there,
Diving quickly through the panic
Like the gulls.
Hai!
Hai!
And the swords were things of beauty
As they glided through the air—
Hai!
Like the gulls.
Hai!

TOWNSPEOPLE

Hai! Hai!
Four black dragons,
Spitting fire!

THIEF	FISHERMAN
And the sun darkened	I had seen
And the sea bubbled	Dragons before,
And the earth trembled	Never so many,
And the sky cracked	Never like these,
And I thought it was the end	And I thought it was the end
Of the world!	Of the world!

THIEF (*Snatching a lacquer box from a bag carried by a fleeing* TOWNSMAN) If I don't take it, the barbarians will. What does it matter, anyway? Whoever these invaders are, they can be no worse than the merchants who have bled us dry, or the samurai who cut us down in the street if we fail to bow when they go by.

(A SAMURAI *enters and surprises the* THIEF, *who drops to his knees and tries to conceal his stolen goods. The* SAMURAI *draws his sword and lops off the* THIEF's *hand*)

GROUP A	GROUP B
And the sun darkened	I had seen
And the sea bubbled	Dragons before,
And the earth trembled	Never so many,
And the sky cracked,	Never like these,
And I thought it was the end	And I thought it was the end
Of the world!	Of the world!

(*Behind the frozen* TOWNSPEOPLE, *the U.S.S.* Powhatan *appears and begins moving ominously Downstage. The* TOWNSPEOPLE *panic and run off in all directions*)

RECITER

And it was.

ACT I

Scene 4

The deck of the U.S.S. Powhatan. SAILORS, *extravagantly stylized like fairy-tale ogres, stand at attention. Behind them, equally bizarre and scary, stand* TWO OFFICERS.

RECITER   They come from a land of mystery behind the setting sun. Barbarians with hooked noses like mountain imps. Giants with wild, coarse hair and faces grey as the dead. Americans! Look how they glare!

(*Suddenly* ALL THE SAILORS *raise their guns and aim them at the audience*)

Look how they aim their sorcerer's weapons directly at us!

(*A sudden spot reveals* COMMODORE MATTHEW CALBRAITH PERRY, *isolated in some conspicuous position on deck. He is a lionlike figure of terror from a child's dream, complete with flowing white mane*)

Oh, look! Their leader! Commodore Matthew Calbraith Perry! Surely he is the King of the Demons come to strike us blind and to devour our children!

(PERRY *makes a sudden, extravagantly threatening gesture*)

In this darkest hour, who will save Japan?

(KAYAMA *appears, crouching in a tiny guard boat which approaches the U.S.S.* Powhatan. *He is so inconspicuous that the* SAILORS *don't even notice him*)

KAYAMA   Please. I am here.

> (*Still no attention*)

Please!

> (*Suddenly one of the* OFFICERS *swivels to him aiming his gun*)

FIRST OFFICER (*Barking.* NOTE: *The* AMERICANS *speak in a terse, stylized pidgin English*)   Boat go! No boats here.

KAYAMA   But—

FIRST OFFICER   Go!

KAYAMA   I will not go. I am the Prefect of Police of the city of Uraga and I say: You must not stay here. Our laws forbid it.

FIRST OFFICER   You hear. I say . . . no boats. Go . . . or . . .

> (*Shouting*)

Bang!

> (*A* SECOND OFFICER, *attracted by the sound, joins him, peering down*)

SECOND OFFICER   What is here?

KAYAMA   Sir, I have orders. You must go away. There is a sacred decree. No foreigner can come to our land.

SECOND OFFICER   What are you?

KAYAMA   I am Prefect of Police for the city of Uraga and I demand that you—

SECOND OFFICER (*Breaking in*)   You . . . policeman?

KAYAMA   Yes, the Prefect of—

SECOND OFFICER   You think officers of great Commodore Payry speak with policeman?

(*Scary guffaw*)

Ha-Ha!

KAYAMA   But I am the representative of the Shogun. I have the authority—

SECOND OFFICER   Americans speak only to great men. Send great man. You hear? Policeman! Ha!

(*Nods to* FIRST OFFICER *and starts away*)

Tell him—off!

FIRST OFFICER (*To* KAYAMA)   Go!

KAYAMA   But—

FIRST OFFICER   Go!
(*Aims gun*)

KAYAMA (*Terrified*)   Ah yes. Excuse me please. Goodbye.

(*He gestures to his* BOATMAN *who starts away. All the* SAILORS *roar with laughter.* KAYAMA *swings back to them, deeply insulted and humiliated*)

Why do they laugh? I do not laugh.

(*More laughter. The boat returns to land where the* SECOND *and* THIRD COUNCILORS *are waiting.* KAYAMA *gets out of the boat and prostrates himself before them*)

SECOND COUNCILOR   You have ordered them to go away?

THIRD COUNCILOR   You have terrified them with the sacred decree?

KAYAMA   I am ashamed, my lords. They will not listen to me. They say they will only speak with a more important personage.

Van Williams

Mako as the Reciter. "Nippon. The Floating Kingdom." *Act One. Scene One.*

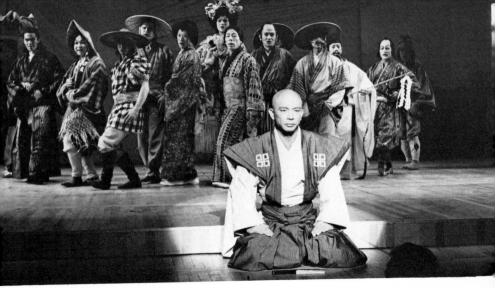

Left: Mako. "The Advantages of Floating in the Middle of the Sea." *Act One. Scene One.*

Below left: Yuki Shimoda as Lord Abe in the Shogun's court. *Act One. Scene One.*

Below: "May the Gods of our fathers make you equal to this awesome task." Lord Abe, center, Kayama (Isao Sato), kneeling, and Tamate (Soon-Teck Oh), left. *Act One. Scene One.*

Tamate, left, and Kayama, right, at home. "Perhaps the foreigners will not come." *Act One. Scene Two.*

"Four black dragons! Spitting fire!" Mark Hsu Syers, Jae Woo Lee, center, and the cast. *Act One. Scene Three.*

Kayama and Manjiro (Sab Shimono) in small boat going to deal with Americans. *Act One. Scene Four.*

"When the Shogun is weak, then the tea must be strong, my Lord."
Act One. Scene Five.

Van Williams

Zoë Dominic

Above: "Kill them!" orders Lord Abe, center, in the Interrogation Scene. *Act One. Scene Six.*

Left: Kayama and Manjiro singing "Poems." *Act One. Scene Six.*

Right: "I own a small commercial venture with a modest clientele. . . ." Ernest Harada as the Madam in "Welcome to Kanagawa." *Act One. Scene Seven.*

Top left: The boy (Gedde Watanabe) and the Old Man (James Dybas) singing "Someone in a Tree." *Act One. Scene Ten.*

Bottom left: American sailors returning from meeting in treaty house. *Act One. Scene Ten.*

Above: Haruki Fujimoto in the "Lion Dance." *Act One. Scene Eleven.*

The court of the Emperor at Kyoto. Left to right, Timm Fujii, Ernest Abuba and Tom Matsusaka. *Act Two. Scene One.*

Martha Swope

"Ah, Detente. . . ." Lord Abe and the Admirals. *Act Two. Scene Two.*

"I don't suppose you'd need a local merchant's help?" quips Conrad Yama to Mako (in hat) upon the introduction of the rickshaw to Japan. *Act Two. Scene Five.*

Martha Swope

Below: "Pretty lady, I'm a million miles from Stepney Green." Left to right, Patrick Kinser-Lau, Freddy Mao (lady), Timm Fujii, Mark Hsu Syers. *Act Two. Scene Six.*

Right: "Conspirator—murderer—fisherman!" Sab Shimono and Isao Sato. *Act Two. Scene Seven.*

Bottom right: Yuki Shimoda as 1976 Japanese businessman in the finale "Next!" *Act Two. Scene Seven.*

All photos: Martha Swope

"Next!" *Act Two. Scene Seven.*

SECOND COUNCILOR You told them you were Prefect of Police?

KAYAMA Yes, my lord, but they only laughed at me. They said:

(*Imitating*)

Americans speak only to great man. I think they mean—

BOTH COUNCILORS (*Appalled*) Us?

KAYAMA Yes, my lords.

BOTH COUNCILORS Impossible!

KAYAMA You needn't go yourselves, my lords. How can barbarians know who is important and who is not? They would assume that anyone dressed in a Councilor's robes—

THIRD COUNCILOR He is right.

SECOND COUNCILOR But who?

KAYAMA My lords, since he has knowledge of their ways, perhaps the shipwrecked fisherman—if he has not yet been disposed of.

THIRD COUNCILOR (*After a beat, beaming*) Summon him at once.

(TWO SUMO WRESTLERS *carry on the cage containing the fisherman* MANJIRO, *and* KAYAMA *crosses to it*)

KAYAMA You have been condemned to death for consorting with foreigners.

MANJIRO Yes, my lord.

KAYAMA You are fortunate. The Shogunate has given me permission to make use of you.

(*To the* SUMO WRESTLERS)

Release the prisoner.

(*The* WRESTLERS *drag* MANJIRO *out of his cage and throw him at* KAYAMA's *feet*)

MANJIRO   I am free, my lord?

KAYAMA   For the time being.

(KAYAMA *turns to lead* MANJIRO *back across the stage*)

MANJIRO (*To one of the* WRESTLERS, *grinning*)   I will miss you.

(KAYAMA *grunts impatiently, and* MANJIRO *dashes across to join him and the* COUNCILORS)

RECITER   The fisherman Manjiro is abruptly promoted and strategies are discussed.

(*To a percussion accompaniment, the* TWO COUNCILORS *and* MANJIRO *mime a stylized, silent, babbling conference. During it, an* ATTENDANT *brings in a splendid robe which is put on* MANJIRO. *The conference abruptly stops.*

KAYAMA *and* MANJIRO *bow to the* COUNCILORS *and go to the guard boat*)

KAYAMA   Remember, hold yourself with great dignity, and not a word! Sit in the bow.

(MANJIRO *nods and takes up his position very grandly.* KAYAMA *stands behind him as the boat returns to the* U.S.S. Powhatan)

KAYAMA (*Calling up to the* FIRST OFFICER)   Please!

FIRST OFFICER (*Barking*)   What?

KAYAMA   I must speak with your officers.

FIRST OFFICER   Why?

KAYAMA   I have returned to present to them a very important dignitary. So if you will call them.

FIRST OFFICER   Busy!

KAYAMA   But I see them standing over there. Please—

MANJIRO (*Breaking in suddenly, with tremendous authority*) Idiot! How dare you plead with petty officers in *my* presence.

(*Gesturing to the* OFFICERS)

You! Here! Come here!

(KAYAMA *gives him a look of appalled horror. From the corner of his mouth, to* KAYAMA)

Don't worry. I know how to handle Americans.

(*Shouting at* OFFICERS)

Man, you hear me. Come, I say.

(*For a beat the* OFFICERS *are bewildered, hesitate, then come down to the rail*)

MANJIRO (*Imperiously to* KAYAMA)   Tell these . . . persons who I am.

KAYAMA (*Bowing to him*)   Oh yes, my lord.

(*To* OFFICERS)

This is the great Councilor, Lord Manjiro, second in power only to the Shogun himself.

MANJIRO (*To* OFFICERS)   Do barbarians not bow to their superiors?

>(*An uncertain glance between the* OFFICERS, *who then give a small bow*)

That is better.

>(*Gesturing towards* PERRY)

Now . . . who is your leader?

SECOND OFFICER   Matthew Calbraith Payry . . . er . . . sir. Commodore. U.S. Navy.

MANJIRO   Tell him to come here.

OFFICERS (*Astounded*)   Tell him?

MANJIRO   Here. To confer with me!

>(*The* TWO OFFICERS *look uneasily at* PERRY, *who turns majestically away*)

SECOND OFFICER   Impossible, sorry. You confer us. We confer Commodore Payry.

MANJIRO   I confer *only* with this Payry.

KAYAMA (*Shocked by this daring, tugging at his sleeve*)   But, my lord—

>(*Whispers in his ear*)

MANJIRO (*Impatiently*)   Very well. For the sake of courtesy, I will make a great concession.

>(*Indicating* PERRY)

He confers with you—

>(*To* OFFICERS)

You confer with *him*—

(*Indicating* KAYAMA)

He confers with *me*.

(*To* KAYAMA)

Ask them why they are here.

KAYAMA   Why are you here?

SECOND OFFICER   We bring greetings and friendly letter from our great President Millyard Fillmore.

MANJIRO   Tell them: Give me the letter and return to America.

KAYAMA   Give the letter to my lord Manjiro, and return to America.

(*The* OFFICERS *go into a very brief, stylized babble conference*)

SECOND OFFICER   Impossible. Letter given only to Emperor.

KAYAMA (*Appalled*)   Emperor!

SECOND OFFICER   Or if against religion, to Shogun.

KAYAMA   Shogun!

SECOND OFFICER   In six days time, you prepare big ceremony. Commodore Payry bring letter. Shogun receive it. Much talk and gifts.

FIRST OFFICER   Six days time. Big ceremony.

(*Pointing to land*)

There!

KAYAMA   But that is impossible! There is a decree, sacred for centuries, which forbids—

MANJIRO (*Breaking in*)   You do not land here. No barbarian sets foot on shore here. You go and tell that to your Payry. Go, I say. Go tell your Payry: All landing—forbidden. Go.

(*The* OFFICERS *hesitate*)

On the double!

(*The* OFFICERS *scurry off to confer with* PERRY)

How'm I doing?

KAYAMA   They seem to be impressed.

MANJIRO   Americans are easy. They shout. You shout louder.

(*Their conference with* PERRY *concluded, the* OFFICERS *come striding back to the rail*)

SECOND OFFICER   You want hear great Commodore Payry's reply to you?

MANJIRO   I will listen.

SECOND OFFICER   Commodore Payry say: Much honored by visit of Japanese Lord. Sends warm greetings.

MANJIRO   I accept his greetings.

SECOND OFFICER   Commodore Payry say: Not to worry. All Japanese customs will be respected in all possible ways.

MANJIRO (*To* KAYAMA)   Didn't I tell you?

SECOND OFFICER   Commodore Payry also say: If big arrangement not made to greet him on land, he turn all cannon on Uraga and blast it off face of earth! !

(*There is a roar of laughter from the* AMERICANS, *as* KAYAMA *and* MANJIRO *fall back in their boat, terrified*)

ACT I

Scene 5

RECITER Enough of these negotiations. It is at last our privilege to encounter Tokugawa Ieyoshi, twelfth direct descendant of the great Tokugawa Ieyasu, unifier of our country, ruling lord of all Japan—the Shogun! And his wife—

(As the RECITER introduces each character, that character makes an entrance down the hanamichi into the SHOGUN's chamber)

his physician, his priests, his soothsayer, his sumo wrestlers, his companion—and his mother. The Shogun!

(The RECITER throws off his RECITER's robes and himself becomes the SHOGUN. He begins rapidly eating rice, grunting. Occasionally, he swills sake. He looks over the rim of the bowl with beady, suspicious eyes at the rest of the room.

His WIFE plays the koto and sings, to no one's pleasure. His MOTHER sits calmly, slowly fanning. A PHYSICIAN brews tea. TWO PRIESTS, TWO SUMO WRESTLERS, A SAMURAI COMPANION and A SOOTHSAYER complete the court)

WIFE (Sings)
Ahhhhhhh . . .

MOTHER (Sings)
My lord . . .

(*He pays no attention*)

WIFE
Ahhhhhhh . . .

MOTHER
My lord . . .

WIFE
Ahhhhhhh . . .

MOTHER (*Loud*)   *Noble* lord . . .

(*He stops eating, startled, looks at her*)

WIFE
Ahhhhhhh . . .

(*The* SHOGUN *gestures her to be quiet*)

MOTHER
It's the Day of the Rat, my lord.
There are four days remaining,
And I see you're entertaining,
But we should have a chat, my lord.
To begin, if I may, my lord,
I've no wish to remind you
But you'll notice just behind you
There are ships in the bay,
They've been sitting there all day
With a letter to convey
And they haven't gone away
And there's every indication
That they're planning to stay, my lord . . .
My lord . . .

(*He looks behind him; the ships glow faintly; he stares, transfixed. He looks at her in alarm; she gestures to the* PHYSICIAN *to bring the tea*)

Have some tea, my lord,
Some chrysanthemum tea.
It's an herb that's superb
For disturbances at sea.

>   (*The* SHOGUN *makes a face at the taste*)

Is the Shogun feeling better?
Good! Now what about this letter?
Is it wise to delay, my lord?
With the days disappearing,
Might we benefit from hearing
What the soothsayers say, my lord? . . .

>   (PHYSICIAN *gets tea from* SHOGUN)

My lord . . . venerable lord . . .

>   (SHOGUN *gestures to* SOOTHSAYER)

SOOTHSAYER (*Comes forward, incants*)

Ahhhhhhh . . .

>   (*Unrolls an astrological chart*)

Wood star . . .
Water star . . .
All celestial omens are—

>   (*The* COURT *holds its breath as he checks*)

Excellent.

>   (*They sigh with relief; he casts an I Ching*)

Deerbones . . .
Turtleshells . . .
Each configuration spells—

>   (*They hold their breath again*)

Victory.

(*They sigh*)

Ahhhhhhh—

(*Whirling and pointing up*)

A spider on the wall!

(WIFE *shrieks*, COURT *is alarmed*)

Signifies success.

(*They relax*)

Whose success I cannot guess . . .

(SHOGUN *grunts disapproval*)

Unless . . .

(*He looks baffled.*

The ships glow ominously as all turn to see them; the SHOGUN *gestures imperiously to the* SUMO WRESTLERS, *who cart the* SOOTHSAYER *away; all change position; the* FESTIVAL DRUM *sounds; a* NEW DAY *begins.*

The SHOGUN *is drawing deeply on a pipe filled with opium*)

WIFE
Ahhhhhhh . . .
Ahhhhhhh . . .

MOTHER
It's the Day of the Ox, my lord.

(WIFE *sings right through her; since the* SHOGUN *doesn't stop her—he's too stoned to hear her—the* MOTHER *does*)

With but three days remaining
And today already waning,
I've a few further shocks, my lord.

(SHOGUN *gives pipe back to* SAMURAI)

To begin, let me say,
At the risk of repetition,
There are ships in the bay,
And they didn't ask permission,
But they sit there all day
In contemptuous array
With a letter to convey
And they haven't gone away
And there's every indication
That they still plan to stay,
And you look a little gray, my lord . . .
My lord . . .

Have some tea, my lord,
Some chrysanthemum tea,
While we plan, if we can,
What our answer ought to be.
If the tea the Shogun drank will
Serve to keep the Shogun tranquil,
I suggest, if I may, my lord,
We consult the Confucians—
They have mystical solutions.
There are none wise as they, my lord . . .

(*The* SHOGUN *has difficulty focusing*)

Over there, my lord . . .

PRIESTS (*Sing*)
Night waters do not break the moon.

That merely is illusion.
The moon is sacred.

No foreign ships can break our laws.
That also is illusion.
Our laws are sacred.

It follows there can be no ships.
They must be an illusion.
Japan is sacred.

> (*Everybody has nodded throughout; they look hope-*
> *fully out at the bay; the ships glow; the* SHOGUN *ges-*
> *tures furiously to the* SUMO WRESTLERS; *the* PRIESTS *are*
> *taken away;* FESTIVAL DRUM; *a* NEW DAY)

WIFE
Ahhhhhhh ...

> (*Her song is sadder, though no less irritating*)

Ahhhhhhh ...

> (*The* SHOGUN *gestures at her weakly to stop*)

MOTHER
It's the Day of the Tiger, my lord.
Only two days remaining,
And I'm tired of explaining
There are ships in the bay
With a letter to convey,
They're on permanent display,
And we must take some position
Or the southern coalition
Will be soon holding sway, my lord ...
And we'll all have to pay, my lord ...

(SHOGUN *gestures weakly*)

Have you something to say, my lord?

(PHYSICIAN *crosses to* SHOGUN)

Have some tea, my lord,
Some chrysanthemum tea.
It's a tangled situation,
As your father would agree.
And it mightn't be so tangled
If you hadn't had him strangled—
But I fear that I stray, my lord.
I've a nagging suspicion
That, in view of your condition,
What we should do is pray, my lord . . .

(*The* SHOGUN *tries weakly to turn away*)

What we should do is pray, my lord.

(*He nods, beaten; the* SAMURAI COMPANION *starts the
prayer*)

SAMURAI COMPANION (*Sings*)
  Blow, wind.
  Great wind.
  Great Kamikaze,
  Winds of the gods.

SAMURAI, SUMO WRESTLERS, PHYSICIAN
  Blow, wind!
  Smite them down!
  Make the invaders dance and drown!

SAMURAI, SUMO WRESTLERS, PHYSICIAN, WIFE, MOTHER
  Blow, wind!

Build the waves!
Hurl the infection
Out of the ocean,
Blow, wind!
Blow, wind!
Blow, wind!

(*They wait for a moment, then look out at the bay;
the ship glows; the* SAMURAI *leaves; the* NEW DAY)

WIFE
Ahhhhhhh . . .

MOTHER
It's the Day of the Rabbit, my lord.
There's but one day remaining,
And beside the fact it's raining,
There are ships in the bay
Which are sitting there today
Just exactly where they sat
On the Day of the Rat—
Oh, and speaking of that, my lord . . .

(SHOGUN *drops*)

My lord—?

(SHOGUN *dies*)

PHYSICIAN   (*Pulling a blanket up over the* SHOGUN's *head*)
The blossom falls on the mountain.
The mountain falls on the blossom.
All things fall—

(SHOGUN *twitches*)

Sometimes.

(The SHOGUN *feebly brings his head out from under the blanket; as soon as his* MOTHER *sees his eyes, she resumes)*

MOTHER

As I started to say:
From that first disturbing day,
When I gave consideration
To this letter they convey,
I decided if there weren't
Any Shogun to receive it,
It would act as a deterrent
Since they'd have no place to leave it,
And they might go away, my lord . . .
Do you see what I say, my lord?

> *(The* PHYSICIAN *offers tea to the* SHOGUN, *who pushes it away as he realizes what it is; his* MOTHER *nods)*

In the tea, my lord,
The chrysanthemum tea—
An informal variation
On the normal recipe.
Though I know my plan had merit,
It's been slow in execution.
If there's one thing you inherit,
It's your father's constitution,
And you're taking so long, my lord . . .

> *(As he sinks)*

Do you think I was wrong, my lord? . . .

> *(He tries to say something)*

No, you must let me speak:

When the Shogun is weak,
Then the tea must be strong, my lord . . .

(*He falls back*)

My Lord—?

(*He dies. The* PHYSICIAN *sings with the* MOTHER)

The blossom falls on the mountain.
The mountain falls on the blossom.
All things—

(*She checks the body*)

Fall.

(*The ships glow again; the* MOTHER *looks at them, smiles and fans; the* SUMO WRESTLERS *and the* PHYSICIAN *and the* WIFE *clear the stage*)

Scene 6

A tableau: KAYAMA *and* MANJIRO *on their knees. On one side, a* SAMURAI *standing guard over them. On the other, an enormous* SUMO WRESTLER *honing a sword on a stone wheel. Upstage of them, posed formally on a low platform,* LORD ABE *and the* TWO COUNCILORS.

ABE   The Americans have not left!

KAYAMA   No, my lord.

ABE   But they have agreed to leave?

KAYAMA   No, my lord.

ABE   Then they have agreed to nothing!

KAYAMA   No, my lord—yes, my lord. My lord, forgive me, but arrangements must be made for the Americans to land and deliver a letter from their President.

SECOND COUNCILOR   Land!

THIRD COUNCILOR   You told them they could come ashore!

ABE   Kill them!

(*The* SUMO WRESTLER *gleefully grinds his sword*)

KAYAMA   Please, my lord, if you will permit me to explain— I have a plan!

ABE   Explain.

KAYAMA My lord, no power on earth can prevent the Americans from landing. But if they were to come ashore—at Kanagawa.

THIRD COUNCILOR (*Astonished*) Kanagawa?

ABE The sacred decree is most specific. It forbids any foreigners to set foot on our soil.

KAYAMA That is why I suggested Kanagawa, my lord. The cove there is quite small. It occurred to me that we could cover all the sand with mats—tatami mats—and build a special treaty house, to receive the letter with courtesy, and many heartfelt promises of a reply.

SECOND COUNCILOR	THIRD COUNCILOR
What?	What does he mean?

ABE (*Silencing them*) And then?

(*The* SUMO WRESTLER *grinds his sword*)

KAYAMA And then? And then—

(*A glance at* MANJIRO)

When the Westerners are satisfied and have departed, we destroy the house and burn the mats and, my lord, neither the decree nor our honor will have been betrayed. The Americans will have come and gone, without setting foot on our sacred soil.

(*For a long moment* ABE *merely stares at him. Then he bursts into laughter. He gestures to the* SUMO WRESTLER, *who reluctantly puts aside his sword*)

ABE Brilliant! Magnificent! Kayama Yesaemon, you will make all necessary arrangements to receive them—as the new *Governor* of the City of Uraga.

KAYAMA   My lord, how can I prove worthy of so great an honor. And yet, dare I ask . . . ?

ABE   Another favor?

KAYAMA   The fisherman Manjiro has been most helpful to me. My lord, if it were possible to revoke his death sentence and attach him to my service—

ABE   He is yours.

(*The* COURT *starts to move off*)

RECITER   If the Councilors can no longer pretend that the Americans are not coming, they have not yet given up the hope of pretending the Americans were never here.

MANJIRO   My Lord Governor of Uraga, you have saved my life.

KAYAMA   And why not, my friend, when you saved mine. The mats were your idea.

MANJIRO   You, a samurai, calling me, a fisherman—friend! This is not Japan. This is America.

KAYAMA   America?

MANJIRO   It is not the Americans who are barbarians. It is us! If you could have seen what I have seen in America—

(*Pause*)

But what I feel in my heart is enough to have me boiled in oil.

KAYAMA   I think you are going to be far too useful to me to boil. But now I must return to Uraga. My wife has had no word from me for many days, and will be worried. Come with me. It is a long journey and we can keep each other company.

(KAYAMA *and* MANJIRO *start the walk to Uraga, "in place," with underscoring*)

I will make a poem.

(*Sings*)

Rain glistening
On the silver birch,
Like my lady's tears.
Your turn.

MANJIRO (*Sings*)
Rain gathering,
Winding into streams,
Like the roads to Boston.
Your turn.

KAYAMA
Haze hovering,
Like the whisper of the silk
As my lady kneels.
Your turn.

MANJIRO
Haze glittering,
Like an echo of the lamps
In the streets of Boston.
Your turn.

KAYAMA
Moon,
I love her like the moon,

Making jewels of the grass
Where my lady walks,
My lady wife.

MANJIRO

Moon,
I love her like the moon,
Washing yesterday away,
As my lady does,
America.
Your turn.

KAYAMA

Wind murmuring.
Is she murmuring for me
Through her field of dreams?
Your turn.

MANJIRO

Wind muttering.
Is she quarreling with me?
Does she want me home?
Your turn.

KAYAMA

I am no nightingale,
But she hears the song
I can sing to her,
My lady wife.

MANJIRO

I am no nightingale,
But my song of her
Could outsing the sea.
America.

KAYAMA

Dawn flickering,
Tracing shadows of the pines
On my lady sleeping.
Your turn.

MANJIRO

Dawn brightening
As she opens up her eyes,
But it's I who come awake.
Your turn.

(*Pause*)

KAYAMA

You go.

(*Pause*)

MANJIRO

Your turn.

(*Pause*)

BOTH

Leaves,
I love her like the leaves,
Changing green to pink to gold,
And the change is everything.
Sun,
I see her like the sun
In the center of a pool,
Sending ripples to the shore,
Till my journey's end.

(KAYAMA's *house appears*)

MANJIRO
  Your turn.

KAYAMA
  Rain.

MANJIRO
  Haze.

KAYAMA
  Moon.

MANJIRO
  Wind.

KAYAMA
  Nightingale.

MANJIRO
  Dawn.

KAYAMA
  Leaves.

MANJIRO
  Sun.

BOTH
  End.

KAYAMA (*Arriving at his house; to* MANJIRO)   Wait here.

    (*He enters the house and approaches* TAMATE)

Tamate, I have the most extraordinary things to tell you!
I have been to Edo and appeared before the Councilors.
You won't believe what happened. I was—

    (*In his excitement* KAYAMA *has not noticed that* TA-

MATE *is still turned away from him in a kneeling position at the household shrine.*

Downstage and below, MANJIRO *waits impatiently, his
attention elsewhere.*

The RECITER *watches the scene*)

Tamate?

(*He walks slowly up behind her and reaches out*)

Tamate. What is it?

(KAYAMA *puts his hand on* TAMATE's *shoulder.*

*She falls into his arms. He appears to cry out, silently.
The appropriate sound comes from the* RECITER. KA-
YAMA *turns her gently around. She is clutching one of
his short swords in her hands, the front of her robes
soaked in blood. He falls to his knees, letting her body
gently to the ground. There is what seems to be an end-
less pause, filled only with the wracked sobbing of the*
RECITER)

MANJIRO (*Impatiently, from outside*)   Kayama!

(*The* RECITER's *sobbing continues*)

KAYAMA (*Woodenly*)   A moment.

(KAYAMA *rises from the floor, moving Downstage. Noticing the blood on his hands, mechanically, he wipes
them clean.*

The RECITER, *still sobbing.*

KAYAMA *joins* MANJIRO, *who is too excited to notice the
change in his friend. He leads him away from the
house, up the hanamichi*)

MANJIRO   My friend, just wait. These Americans may be
tough and impolite, but they are the most amazing people.
You'll see. Their coming here is the best thing that ever
happened to Japan.

> (As MANJIRO *and* KAYAMA *make their way up the hana-
> michi, they are passed by a garish, middle-aged* MADAM
> *coming down*)

ACT I

Scene 7

The MADAM *looks impatiently back over her shoulder at* FOUR GIRLS *who are following her, with some reluctance, down toward the stage.*

MADAM   Hurry up, girls, for goodness' sake. The Americans will have already landed.

> (*Sings, to the audience*)

I own a small commercial venture
With a modest clientele
In Kanagawa.

GIRLS (*Sing, in tandem*)
I think I see one over there behind the trees!

MADAM
Sh!

> (*To the audience*)

It's been my family's for centuries
And doing very well—
For Kanagawa.

GIRLS   (*In tandem*)
I hear they're covered all with hair, like some disease.

MADAM
Sh!

GIRLS
Except their knees.

MADAM
  Sh!

          (*To the audience*)

  The arrival of these giants
  Out of the blue,
  Bringing panic to my clients,
  Alters my view.
  With so many of them fleeing,
  Conferring, decreeing,
  I find myself agreeing
  With the ancient haiku:

RECITER
  The nest-building bird,
  Seeing the tree without twigs,
  Looks for new forests.

MADAM   Exactly.

          (*A "forest" of bamboo poles, carried on by* STAGEHANDS,
          forms on stage. The MADAM *searches through it.*)

  Yo-ho! Americans!

GIRLS (*Also searching*)
  Yo-ho! Americans!

MADAM
  Welcome to Kanagawa.

GIRLS (*Raucously*)
  Welcome to Kanagawa!

MADAM
  No . . .

          (*Delicately*)

  Welcome to Kanagawa.

GIRLS
Oh...

(*Imitating*)

Welcome to Kanagawa.

MADAM
So...

(*As the* GIRLS *continue singing softly*)

With all my flowers disappearing
In alarm,
I've been reduced to commandeering
From the farm.

(*Shrugs*)

But with appropriate veneering,
Even green wood has its charm.

GIRLS   (*Searching*)
Yo-ho!
Yo-ho!

MADAM   (*Beckoning them*)
Yo-ho!

(*As* MUSIC *continues under, the* MADAM *hands out "instructional" fans; as each* GIRL *opens her fan, she giggles in embarrassment or excitement at the erotic drawings which cover it; the* FOURTH GIRL *cries*)

MADAM   (*Pointing to the* FIRST GIRL's *fan*)
That you'll have to bend for—
Can you see why?

(FIRST GIRL *giggles and goes to forest, calling*)

FIRST GIRL
  Yo-ho!

MADAM   (*Points to* SECOND GIRL'*s fan*)
  That you'll need a friend for—
  Still, you might try.

SECOND GIRL   (*Similarly*)
  Yo-ho!

MADAM   (*Points to* THIRD GIRL'*s fan*)
  That you do *through* the kimono—
  Not very much.

THIRD GIRL   (*Similarly*)
  Yo-ho!

MADAM   (*Points to* FOURTH GIRL'*s fan*)
  That you use glue, then you—

        (*As* FOURTH GIRL *points to spot on fan*)

  No, no, no, no,
  Those you don't touch!

ALL
  Welcome to Kanagawa,
  Music and food for twenty yen—
  Music and food—

MADAM
  And maybe then—

ALL
  Welcome!

GIRLS
  Welcome to Kanagawa!

MADAM
Low...

GIRLS   (*Lowering their voices*)
Welcome to Kanagawa.

MADAM
So...

(*The* GIRLS *continue singing underneath*)

You must neither be too wary
Nor too bold,
As there's no telling with barbarians,
I'm told,
Because not only are they hairy,
But extremely uncontrolled.

GIRLS   (*Excited*)
Yo-ho!

MADAM   (*Beckoning them*)
Yo-ho!

(*To* FIRST GIRL, *pointing to fan*)

That you mustn't wash for,
Not till you're done.

FIRST GIRL
Yo-ho!

MADAM   (*To* SECOND GIRL, *similarly*)
That you use a squash for—
Or pumpkins are fun.

SECOND GIRL
Yo-ho!

MADAM   (*To* THIRD GIRL)
That you do slow-

Ly and gently—
Don't take a chance.

THIRD GIRL
   Yo-ho!

MADAM   (*To* FOURTH GIRL)
   That they don't know
   About, evidently—
   Get an advance.

ALL
   Welcome to Kanagawa!
   Music and food and company!
   Music and food—

MADAM
   —and for a fee—

ALL
   Welcome!

      (DANCE—*during which the* FOURTH GIRL *blunders diz-
      zily*)

MADAM (*Furiously*)   Back to the farm!

      (GIRL *starts off disconsolately;* MADAM *stops her*)

Tomorrow!

      (*To audience*)

When a country is in trouble,
Choices are few.
And apart from charging double,
What can you do?
With my clients off defending,
And strangers descending,

I find myself depending
On the ancient haiku:

RECITER

The bird from the sea,
Not knowing pine from bamboo,
Roosts on anything.

MADAM

Exactly.

(DANCE)

GIRLS

Welcome to Kanagawa!

MADAM

Flow!

GIRLS (*Flowing*)   Welcome to Kanagawa!

MADAM

Glow!

GIRLS (*Glowing*)   Welcome to Kanagawa!

MADAM

Grow!

GIRLS (*Loudly*)   Welcome to Kanagawa!

MADAM (*Like a general to her troops*)   Go!

GIRLS

Welcome to Kanagawa! Yo-ho!
Welcome to Kanagawa! Yo-ho!

(*Repeated, until first the* GIRLS *and then the* MADAM
have exited)

ACT I

Scene 8

The TWO AMERICAN OFFICERS *appear Stage Right, the* FIRST OFFICER *reading from a list.*

FIRST OFFICER   . . . carbines, revolvers, army pistols, assorted cartridges and shot, fifteen Hall's rifles, three Maynard's muskets, and two dozen cavalry swords and bayonets.

(AMERICAN SAILORS *carry these items on and pile them Stage Right*)

RECITER   To smooth the way for the American landing at Kanagawa, Commodore Perry has insisted on delivering to the Councilors several presents, as a demonstration of his friendship and good will. And to show us what we stand to gain from trading with his countrymen.

FIRST OFFICER   One barrel whiskey. One basket champagne. One cask cherry cordial. A bathtub and a parlor stove.

(As AMERICAN SAILORS *continue to carry on the American gifts, the* TWO JAPANESE COUNCILORS *enter from Stage Left and supervise the laying out of a small tea table on which a few exquisitely wrapped packages are placed*)

RECITER   Not to be outdone, the Councilors have arranged their gifts for the Westerners. Each one, carefully selected, reflects some aspect of our craftsmanship and culture.

FIRST OFFICER   One collection lithographs, depicting steamships, elephants, and the city of New Orleans. Two batteries, two bags Irish potatoes. Three boxes books containing among other volumes, Audubon's "Birds of America," Audubon's "Quadrupeds," Bancroft's "History of the United States," Downing's "Connecticut Country Houses," Owen's "Geology of Minnesota," Roget's "Thesaurus," and a complete list of United States Post Offices.

(*The* OFFICERS *now stand next to an enormous pile of boxes and cases*)

RECITER   That is all?

SECOND OFFICER   For now. The rest will be delivered this afternoon, along with six hundred yards of telegraph cable, the fire engine, and the working locomotive.

RECITER   Your generosity is overwhelming.

SECOND OFFICER   Yes.

SECOND COUNCILOR   (*Indicating the delicate Japanese gifts*) Our offerings are small.

THIRD COUNCILOR   We hope that they will give you pleasure.

(*The* AMERICAN OFFICERS *nod skeptically.* AMERICAN SAILORS *enter, pick up the Japanese gifts, and follow the* OFFICERS *off. Two* SUMO WRESTLERS *then enter, lift the American presents off the floor with ease, and carry them away*)

ACT I

Scene 9

A SAMURAI *enters holding up to his face an* OLD MAN's *mask.*

SAMURAI   The Americans insisted that their mission was a peaceful one. But because we did not know if we could trust them, we chose a samurai whose task it was to muster our defenses. And that samurai . . .

(*Dropping the mask and emerging as a* YOUNGER MAN)

—was me. I ordered canvas screens to be stretched across the cliffs at Kanagawa.

(STAGEHANDS *enter with a strip of canvas which indicates the screens*)

Behind the screens, I was able to conceal—five thousand armored swordsmen—

(*Below the screen appear the legs of the* SWORDSMEN)

—carrying enormous bows—

(*The tips of the bows appear above the screen*)

—all of them on horseback!

(*The legs disappear and are replaced by hooves*)

A most impressive force—and with the canvas masking them our enemy might think that twice, three times that many warriors were assembled. At least that's what we thought. But when the Americans saw our screens they called out from their ships. "Pull down those drapes. What kind of army hides behind a parlor curtain!" And then—they roared with laughter.

(*He draws his sword in frustration, then slams it back in its sheath*)

Most discouraging. I mean, what are you going to do with people like that?

(*The* SAMURAI *bows and exits, raising the* OLD MAN'S *mask back up to his face and chanting his opening lines.*

The SCREEN *follows him*)

ACT I

Scene 10

RECITER   From the personal journal of Commodore Matthew Calbraith Perry. 14 July, 1853. As I supervise the final preparations for this afternoon's historic landing at Kanagawa, I am moved to hope the Japanese will voluntarily accept the reasonable and pacific overtures embodied in our friendly letter. Should I hope in vain, however, should these backward, semibarbarous people be reluctant to forsake their policy of isolation, then I stand prepared to introduce them into the community of civilized nations by whatever means are necessary. It is my understanding that this preposterous empire has been closed to foreigners for over two hundred and fifty years, and I for one feel that that has been more than long enough!

> (*The Treaty House at Kanagawa is assembled Onstage. Festive kites are lowered from the flies, a tree is rolled on—the stage is set for the* AMERICANS' *arrival.* ABE, *the* SECOND COUNCILOR, KAYAMA *and several* SAMURAI *emerge from the house and stare up the hanamichi*)

SECOND COUNCILOR   They are late. It is an insult.

ABE   Where is the warrior?

KAYAMA   Here, my lord!

> (KAYAMA *slides back a panel in the base of the house, revealing a* SAMURAI *hidden under the floorboards*)

69

ABE   He understands the signal?

KAYAMA   Yes, my lord. If the Westerners should draw their weapons, I will knock twice and he will come up through the floor and cut them down.

SECOND COUNCILOR   Pity the Americans if they should draw their guns.

> (*The sound of an American march from the rear of the hanamichi*)

They come!

ABE   Inside!

> (ABE *and the* SECOND COUNCILOR *disappear inside the Treaty House. Simultaneously, a* SAMURAI *appears at the rear of the hanamichi, rolling straw matting down toward the stage. Behind him comes the American landing party: a marching* BAND, *a row of* ENLISTED MEN, *the* TWO AMERICAN OFFICERS, *and finally* PERRY *himself. The* ENLISTED MEN *form ranks outside the house, while* PERRY *and the* OFFICERS *are escorted inside*)

RECITER   No one knows what was said behind the shutters of the Treaty House. The Shogun's Councilors kept their story secret, and though the Westerners have their own official version—I would not believe a word of it. What a shame that there is no authentic Japanese account of what took place on that historic day.

> (*An* OLD JAPANESE MAN *carrying an attaché case enters*)

OLD MAN (*Sings*)
Pardon me, I was there.

RECITER (*Sings*)
You were where?

OLD MAN
At the Treaty House.

RECITER
At the Treaty House?

OLD MAN
There was a tree . . .

RECITER
Which was where?

OLD MAN
Very near.

RECITER   (*Indicating*)
Over here?

OLD MAN   (*Indicating*)
Maybe over there,
But there were trees then, everywhere.
May I show you?

RECITER
If you please.

OLD MAN
There were trees
Then, everywhere . . .

RECITER
But you were there.

OLD MAN
And I was there!
Let me show you.

RECITER
If you please.

OLD MAN

I was younger then . . .

(*Tries to climb; defensively*)

I was good at climbing trees . . .

(*Tries again; apologetically*)

I was younger then . . .

(*Again*)

I saw everything.
I was hidden all the time . . .

(*Again*)

It was easier to climb . . .

(*Again*)

I was younger then.

(*Again*)

I saw everything!

(*Again*)

Where they came and where they went—
I was part of the event.
I was someone in a tree.

(*Again, now desperate*)

I was younger then!

(*Suddenly a* YOUNG BOY *appears, scurries across stage and up the tree*)

BOY   (*Triumphantly, to the* OLD MAN)
Tell him what I see!

OLD MAN (*To* RECITER)
    I am in a tree.
    I am ten.
    I am in a tree.

BOY (*Sings, to* RECITER)
    I was younger then.

OLD MAN
    In between the eaves I can see—

        (*To* BOY)

    Tell me what I see.

        (*To* RECITER)

    I was only ten.

BOY   (*Peering into the Treaty House*)
    I see men and matting.
    Some are old, some chatting.

OLD MAN
    If it happened, I was there!

BOTH
    I saw (see) everything!

OLD MAN
    I was someone in a tree.

BOY
    Tell him what I see.

OLD MAN
    Some of them have gold on their coats.

BOY   (*Correcting him*)
    One of them has gold.

(*To the* RECITER)

He was younger then.

OLD MAN
Someone crawls around, passing notes—

BOY
Someone very old—

OLD MAN (*To the* RECITER)
He was only ten.

BOY
And there's someone in a tree—

OLD MAN
—or the day is incomplete.

BOTH
Without someone in a tree,
Nothing happened here.

OLD MAN
I am hiding in a tree.

BOY
I'm a fragment of the day.

BOTH
If I weren't, who's to say
Things would happen here the way
That they happened here?

OLD MAN
I was there then.

BOY
I am here still.
It's the fragment, not the day.

OLD MAN
It's the pebble, not the stream.

BOTH
It's the ripple, not the sea,
Not the building but the beam,
Not the garden but the stone,
Not the Treaty House,
Someone in a tree.

WARRIOR   (*Slides panel open underneath the house, sings*)
If you please, I am also here—
Pardon me, I am here.

(*The* OTHERS *pay no attention*)

OLD MAN
They kept drinking cups of tea.

BOY
They kept sitting on the floor.

OLD MAN
They drank many cups of tea.

BOTH   (*To* EACH OTHER)
No, we told him that before.

WARRIOR
If you please, I am here.

RECITER   (*Noticing*)
You are where?

WARRIOR
In the Treaty House.

RECITER
In the Treaty House?

WARRIOR
  Or very near.

RECITER
  Can you hear?

WARRIOR
  I'm below.

RECITER
  So I notice.

WARRIOR
  Underneath the floor,
  And so I can't see anything.

RECITER
  Can you hear?

WARRIOR
  I can hear them,
  But I can't see anything.

RECITER
  But you can hear?

WARRIOR
  But I can hear.
  Shall I listen?

RECITER
  If you please.

WARRIOR
  I can hear them now . . .

    (*Pressing his ear closer*)

  I shall try to shift my knees . . .

(*He does*)

I can hear them now . . .

(*Obviously not hearing*)

I hear everything!
I'm the part that's underneath,
With my sword inside my sheath.

(*Listening again*)

I can hear them now . . .

(*Again*)

One is over me.
If they knock, then I appear!
I'm a part of what I hear!
I'm the fragment underneath!

(*Listening, triumphantly*)

I can hear them now!

RECITER, OLD MAN, BOY
Tell us what you hear!

WARRIOR
First I hear a creak and a thump.
Now I hear a clink . . .
Then they talk a bit . . .
Many times they shout when they speak.
Other times they think.
Or they argue it . . .
I hear floorboards groaning . . .
Angry growls . . . much droning . . .
Since I hear them, they are there!

As they argue it,
I'm the listener underneath.

BOY   (*Peering into the House*)
Someone reads a list
From a box.

WARRIOR   (*Listening*)
Someone talks of laws.

OLD MAN
Then they fan a bit.

BOY
Someone bangs a fist.

WARRIOR
Someone knocks.

OLD MAN
Now there was a pause.

ALL
Then they argue it:

WARRIOR
"But we want . . ."
"No, you can't and we won't . . ."
"But we need it and we want . . ."
"Will you grant—? . . . If you don't . . ."
"We concede it . . ."

OLD MAN	WARRIOR	BOY
And they sat	I can hear	
Through the night	them.	
And they lit		
Yellow tapers.		

I was	I'm a	And they
There	Fragment of the	Chat
Then.	Day.	And they fight
		And they sit
		Signing papers.
If I	If I	I am
Weren't, who's to	Weren't, who's to	There
Say	Say	Still.
Things would	Things would	If I
Happen here the	Happen here the	Weren't, who's to
Way	Way	Say
That they're	That they're	That they're
Happening?	Happening?	Happening?

ALL

It's the fragment, not the day.
It's the pebble, not the stream.
It's the ripple, not the sea
That is happening.
Not the building but the beam,
Not the garden but the stone,
Only cups of tea
And history
And someone in a tree.

(*The* WARRIOR *slides his panel closed. The* OLD MAN *and* BOY *exit*)

RECITER Whatever happened behind the shutters of the Treaty House, Kayama Yesaemon's plan was a success. The letter was delivered. The Americans were satisfied. And they left.

(*The* AMERICAN OFFICERS *emerge from the House, followed by* ABE *and his* RETAINERS. *Bows are exchanged,*

then the OFFICERS *lead the* AMERICAN ENLISTED MEN
back up the hanamichi)

ABE (*To his* RETAINERS) Quickly there, nothing must remain!

(*The Treaty House is dismantled, and the stage is
cleared*)

RECITER We tore down the house and rolled up the mats,
taking great care that the contaminated side should not
touch the ground. Once again, all was as it had been. The
barbarian threat had forever been removed. Ha!

Scene 11

Suddenly the lion-like figure of COMMODORE PERRY *leaps out Onstage and performs a strutting, leaping dance of triumph.*

ACT II

Scene 1

The RECITER *enters and kneels at the side of the stage. A* MUSICIAN *plays the shamisen and sings. A* STAGEHAND *runs the show curtain across the stage, revealing the Imperial Court in Kyoto—the puppet/*EMPEROR, *a* PRIEST, *and* TWO *bored* NOBLES *playing cat's cradle.*

RECITER The spiritual heart of all Japan—the court of the Emperor at Kyoto, the palace of the living god descended from the sun itself, the throne room of the sacred ruler of the Islands of Nippon!

(*The* PRIEST *unfurls a roll of rice paper covered with calligraphy.* LORD ABE *and the* COUNCILORS *enter, followed by* KAYAMA *and* MANJIRO)

Of course, a thousand years ago the Emperor's power was wrested from him by the warlord called the Shogun, and since that time the Emperor has ruled in name alone. But ancient duties still must be discharged. Observe how low Lord Abe bows down to the ruler whom he rules.

(ABE *prostrates himself before the puppet/*EMPEROR. *The* PRIEST *picks up the sticks which manipulate the puppet's arms and holds them out. The* NOBLES *pause in their game and listen*)

His holiness the Emperor speaks.

82

PRIEST (*Speaking for the* EMPEROR, *manipulating the puppet's arms*) The Americans did not come. Had the Americans come, the honor of Japan and the sanctity of its ancestral soil would have been defiled. But the Americans did not come. Therefore . . . the Emperor formally acknowledges Lord Abe Masahiro as the thirteenth Tokugawa Shogun of the Empire of Japan.

> (ABE *bows curtly*)

The Emperor formally acknowledges Kayama Yesaemon as Governor of the city of Uraga.

> (KAYAMA *bows curtly*)

The Emperor formally rescinds the sentence of death imposed upon the fisherman Manjiro—

> (MANJIRO *bows curtly*)

And elevates him to the rank of samurai.

> (MANJIRO *snaps his head up in surprise, then quickly lowers it again.* ATTENDANTS *enter, carrying robes and swords. They raise* MANJIRO *off the floor and drape him in a robe which bears his new family crest. Next the* ATTENDANTS *produce two swords and strap them around* MANJIRO's *waist. With great ceremony they proceed to shave his shaggy wig, leaving only a samurai's topknot at the back. For a moment* MANJIRO *stands transfixed, then he falls back to his knees and prostrates himself before the* EMPEROR)

PRIEST (*Grandly*) The Emperor congratulates the saviors of Japan—

> (ABE, *the* COUNCILORS, KAYAMA *and* MANJIRO *bow*)

And respectfully suggests that his monthly allowance of incense is inadequate.

FIRST NOBLE   The Emperor respectfully suggests that his monthly allowance of ink is inadequate.

SECOND NOBLE   The Emperor respectfully suggests that his monthly allowance of yarn is inadequate.

ABE   As the Emperor knows, there are many even more important claims on our resources. But the Shogunate will certainly consider any reasonable requests.

RECITER   A haiku: The hand which feeds it grudgingly
Is the first hand
Which the dog will bite.

(*He smiles*)

If it ever gets the chance.

PRIEST (*Speaking for the* EMPEROR)   The Emperor smiles on his loyal subjects and permits them to depart—secure in the knowledge that the barbarian threat has forever been removed.

(LORD ABE *backs out of the Court and is isolated from it by a curtain which drops behind his back*)

ABE   Goodbye America. Come back in two hundred fifty years!

(*He laughs*)

ACT II

Scene 2

ABE *is surprised by the sudden sound of a marching band. An* AMERICAN ADMIRAL *enters down the hana-michi, carrying a plaque and some official documents.*

AMERICAN ADMIRAL (*Sings, to* ABE)
Please hello, America back,
Commodore Perry say hello.
Also comes memorial plaque
President Fillmore wish bestow.

Emperor read our letter? If no,
Commodore Perry very sad.
Emperor like our letter? If so,
Commodore Perry very merry,
President Fillmore still more glad.

Last time we visit, too short.
This time we visit for slow.
Last time we come, come with warships,
Now with more ships—
Say hello!
This time request use of port,
Port for commercial intention,
Harbor with ample dimension.

ABE (*Sings*)
But you can't—

85

AMERICAN ADMIRAL
Only one
Little port
For a freighter.

ABE
But you can't—

AMERICAN ADMIRAL
Just for fun,
Be a sport.

ABE
Maybe later—

AMERICAN ADMIRAL
But we bring many recent invention:
Kerosene
And cement
And a grain
Elevator,
A machine
You can rent
Called a "train"—

ABE
—Maybe later—

AMERICAN ADMIRAL
—Also cannon to shoot
Big loud salute,
Like so:

> (*An* EXPLOSION *offstage.* LIGHT *flashes.* ABE *cowers in
> fear, accepts the document*)

Say hello!

(EXPLOSION. ABE *takes the pen and signs*)

Treaty meet approval? If no,
Commodore Perry very fierce.
Disregard confusion below:
President Fillmore now name Pierce.

(*Whisking the paper away and blowing on it to dry the ink*)

Good! At last agreement is made,
Letter will let us come again.
First result of mutual trade:
Commodore getting letter letting,

(*Gesturing to* ABE *to keep the pen as a souvenir*)

Councilor getting fancy pen!
Goodbye.

(*Bows;* ABE *bows back*)

Goodbye.

ABE

Goodbye.

(*Bows;* ADMIRAL *bows back*)

AMERICAN ADMIRAL

Goodbye.

ABE

Goodbye.

AMERICAN ADMIRAL

Please goodbye.

(*Bows;* ABE *bows back*)

BRITISH ADMIRAL *(Appearing suddenly)*
Hello!

AMERICAN ADMIRAL *(To ABE)*
Goodbye.

> *(Bows; the BRITISH ADMIRAL bows in greeting; ABE is confused, bows halfway between them)*

BRITISH ADMIRAL
Hello, please!

AMERICAN ADMIRAL
Goodbye.

> *(ALL THREE bow again; the AMERICAN ADMIRAL retires to one side and studies the treaty)*

BRITISH ADMIRAL *(In unflappable Gilbert-and-Sullivan style, sings to ABE)*
Please
Hello, I come with letters from Her Majesty Victoria
Who, learning how you're trading now, sang "Hallelujah, Gloria!"
And sent me to convey to you her positive euphoria
As well as little gifts from Britain's various emporia.

> *(Offers a tin of tea to ABE)*

RECITER
The man has come with letters from Her Majesty Victoria
As well as little gifts from Britain's various emporia.

ABE
Tea?

BRITISH ADMIRAL *(Patiently)*
For drink.

ABE

I see.

I thank you—

BRITISH ADMIRAL

I think

Her letters do contain a few proposals to your Emperor

Which if, of course, he won't endorse, will put her in a
temper or,

More happily, should he agree, will serve to keep her placid,
or

At least till I am followed by a permanent ambassador.

(*Waves some documents about*)

RECITER

A treaty port and, from the Court, a permanent ambassador.

A treaty port and, from the Court, a permanent ambassador.

A treaty port and, from the Court, a permanent ambassador.

And more.

BRITISH ADMIRAL

Her Majesty considers the arrangements to be tentative

Until we ship a proper diplomatic representative.

We don't foresee that you will be the least bit argumenta-
tive,

So please ignore the man-of-war we brought as a preventative.

RECITER

Yes, please ignore the man-of-war

That's anchored rather near to shore.

It's nothing but a metaphor

That acts as a preventative.

(*Another enormous* EXPLOSION *offstage; again light flashes; again* ABE *blinks and reaches for the documents*)

BRITISH ADMIRAL

All clear?

Just so.

Sign here.

(*As* ABE *starts to sign, the* AMERICAN ADMIRAL *returns*)

AMERICAN ADMIRAL

Hello, hello, objection, resent!

President Pierce say "moment's pause."

British get ambassador sent,

President Pierce get extra clause.

(*As he presents more papers to* ABE, *the* DUTCH ADMIRAL *appears. He is a Dutch comic, Weber-and-Fields style, complete with Hans Brinker pockets and heavy clogs. He dances a waltz-clog continually while he sings*)

DUTCH ADMIRAL

Vait! Please hello!

Don't forget ze Dutch!

Like to keep in touch!

Zank you very much!

Tell zem to go,

Button up ze lips.

Vot do little nips

Vant vit battleships?

(*Dances briefly, withdraws a tulip, waves it enticingly at* ABE)

Hold everyzing!

Ve gonna bring

Chocolate!
Vouldn't you like to lease
A beautiful liddle piece
Of chocolate?
Listen, zat's not to mention
Vunderful—pay attention!—
Vindmills
Und tulips,

> (*Gives* ABE *the tulip*)

Und vouldn' you like a vooden shoe?

> (*Gives* ABE *documents*)

Zere—can you read?
Good! Ve vill need
Two ports,
Vun of zem not too rocky—
How about Nagasaki?—
Two ports,
Vun of zem for ze cocoa—
Vot do you call it?—Yoko-
Hama! Ja!
Und Nagasaki! Ja!
Sign here!

> (*Dances, making semaphore signals to the sea.*
>
> *Another* EXPLOSION.
>
> *The* DUTCH ADMIRAL *settles on the floor in front of*
> ABE, *with his back to the audience.*
>
> *The* AMERICAN *and* BRITISH ADMIRALS *cross to* ABE *si-*
> *multaneously.*
>
> *Simultaneously:*)

AMERICAN ADMIRAL
Wait please, objection again!
Dutch getting too many seaports.
President now wanting *three* ports—

BRITISH ADMIRAL
Great Britain wishes her position clear and indisputable:
We're not amused at being used and therefore stand immutable.
And though you Japs are foxy chaps and damnably inscrutable—

> (*The* RUSSIAN ADMIRAL *appears at the rear of the hanamichi. He is very tired and soulful and not terribly interested in the job at hand; he wears a fancy coat*)

RUSSIAN ADMIRAL (*Sings*)
Please hello . . .

DUTCH ADMIRAL   (*To the other* ADMIRALS)
Vait! Please hello!
Comes ze monkey wrench!
Smell dot awful stench:
Probably ze French.

AMERICAN ADMIRAL   (*Paying no attention, to* ABE)
—Also insist giving free ports—

BRITISH ADMIRAL   (*Ditto, simultaneously*)
—Reviewing it from where we sit, the facts are irrefutable—

RUSSIAN ADMIRAL
Please hello . . .

DUTCH ADMIRAL
Ach, nein, of course,
My mistake, ze Czar.

Smell ze caviar—
Leave ze door ajar.

AMERICAN ADMIRAL   (*As above*)
—Also want annual Reports—

BRITISH ADMIRAL   (*Ditto*)
—And thus, in short, a single port is patently unsuitable!

RUSSIAN ADMIRAL   (*Loudly*)
Please hello,
Is bringing Czar's request,
Braving snow
With letter to protest:
Since we know
You trading with the West,
You might at least
(Don't touch the coat!)
Start looking east—

        (*Thinking about it*)

—or closer west—

        (*Thinking again*)

—well, farther north—

        (*Looking around*)

Are we the fourth?
I feel depressed.
(Don't touch the coat!).

        (*Pulling himself together unhappily, to* ABE, *presenting documents.* ABE *is now inundated*)

Coming next
Is extraterritoriality.

Noting text
Say "Extraterritoriality."
You perplexed
By "Extraterritoriality"?

(*Points*)

Just noting clause
(Don't touch the coat!)
Which say your laws
Do not apply
(Don't touch the coat!)
When we drop by—
Not getting shot,
No matter what:
A minor scrape,
A major rape,
And we escape
(Don't touch the cape!)
That's what is extraterritoriality.

(*Sighs*)

Fair is fair—
You wish perhaps to vote?
What we care
You liking what we wrote?

(*Points to sea*)

Sitting there
Is finest fleet afloat.
Observing boat?

(*Smiles.*

Another enormous EXPLOSION.

He stands imperturbably, lowering his eyes in silent resignation as ABE *instinctively leans forward to cling to him in terror*)

Don't touch the coat.

(*Another* EXPLOSION)

Just sign the note.

(*As* ABE *signs,* ALL THE OTHER ADMIRALS *sing simultaneously, to* ABE:)

BRITISH ADMIRAL

The British feel these latest dealings verge on immorality.
The element of precedent imperils our neutrality.
We're rather vexed, your giving extraterritoriality.
We must insist you offer this to every nationality!

DUTCH ADMIRAL

Ve vant de same
Vot de Russkies claim!
Vhy you let them came?
Dirty rotten shame!

AMERICAN ADMIRAL

U.S.A. extremely upset!
President Pierce say solid "No!"

FRENCH ADMIRAL (*Appears simultaneously—he is a dandy, disgustingly gay and charming*)
'Allo!—

(*No one pays attention*)

Please 'allo!

(*Again—loudly*)

Please 'allo!

(*They all look—he smiles broadly*)

'Allo! 'Allo! 'Allo!

(*Blows them all a kiss and sings*)

I bring word, I bring word
From Napoleon ze Third.
'E 'ad 'eard what 'ave occurred 'ere
From ze little bird!
Undeterred, we conferred,
Though we felt zat we'd been slurred,
And ze verdict was he spurred
Me 'ere to bring ze word!
Would you like to know ze word
From Napoleon ze Third?

(*Shoves a bundle of papers at* ABE)

It's detente! Oui, detente!
Zat's ze only thing we want!
Just detente! Ooh, detente!
No agreement could be more fair!
Signing pacts, passing acts,
Zere's no time for making warfare
When you're always busy making wiz ze
Mutual detente!

(*Blows another kiss*)

A detente, a detente
Is ze only thing we wish!
Same as zem, except additional
Ze rights to fish!
You'll be paid, you'll be paid,

And we'll 'ave ze big parade
If we somehow can persuade
You to accept our aid.

> (*Gestures to the sea*—

> A *stylized bass-drum* EXPLOSION)

It is not to be afraid ...

> (*Another one*)

As we only wish to trade ...

> (*As he smiles to reassure* ABE, *the biggest* EXPLOSION *yet
> —it is practically the atom bomb.* ABE *hastily starts to
> sign, which causes the others to throw more papers at
> him*)

FRENCH ADMIRAL   (*Gaily*)
   Ah, detente! Oui, detente!
   Zat's ze only thing we want!
   Leave ze grain, leave ze train,
   Put champagne among your imports!
   Tell each man zat Japan
   Can't be bothered giving him ports
   While she's in a tizzy,
   Dizzy wiz ze
   Mutual detente!

ABE   (*Pleading to him*)
   It is late,
   And I fear—
   Well, you see,
   There's a famine ...
   Could you wait

For a year?
We'll agree to
Examine
It—

FRENCH ADMIRAL   (*Gaily dancing, paying no attention, simul-*
taneously)
A detente! A detente!
Zat's ze only thing we want!

(*And now* EVERYBODY *sings simultaneously*)

ABE (*To each in turn*)
—But lat-
Er, I fear.
There's a drought
And a famine . . .   FRENCH ADMIRAL
If you wait   Just detente! Oooh, detente!
For a year,   No agreement could be more fair!
Then no doubt   Signing pacts, passing acts,
We'll examine   Zere's no time for making warfare.
It, but we've   Why discuss, make ze fuss,
Had a quake   Since ze West belong to us?
And a flood   And ze East we have leased for ze
And a famine . . .   French administration.
Please believe   If you force in ze Norce,
We will take   Zen we burn ze Dutch legation.
It to stud-
Y, examine
It, but please,
If you'll wait
For a year . . .
There's a famine . . .

DUTCH ADMIRAL

Vait please hallo!
Don't forget ze Dutch!
Ve vant just as much
Fishing rights and such!
Tell zem to go,
Othervise ve post
Battleships at most
Ports along ze coast.
You can have ze Vest,
Ve vill take ze rest.

BRITISH ADMIRAL

One moment, please, I think that
    these assure us exclusivity
For Western ports and other sorts of
    maritime activity,
And if you mean to intervene, as is
    the Dutch proclivity,
We'll blow you nits to little bits,
    with suitable festivity.

AMERICAN ADMIRAL

Wait please, hello, West is ours.
Wait please, the East is the best coast.
We'll trade you two on the West coast.

RUSSIAN ADMIRAL

Please hello, no seaports on the West.
United States too near to Czar,
Is tempting fates, is go too far
(Don't touch the coat!)

ALL THE ADMIRALS   (*Doing the CanCan, to* ABE)

Ah, detentes! Ah, detentes!
They're what everybody wants!
You should want a detente—
Makes a nation like a brother!
We'll be here every year
To protect you from each other
And to see you aren't
Signing foreign
Treaties and detentes!

Please hello! We must go,
But our intercourse will grow
Through detente, as detente
Brings complete cooperation.
By the way, may we say
We adore your little nation,
And with heavy cannon
Wish you an un-
Ending please hello! ! !

ACT II

Scene 3

The Imperial Court. The puppet/EMPEROR has aged somewhat, but he is still surrounded by his retinue— the PRIEST and the TWO NOBLES, who are still engaged with their knitting and calligraphy.

RECITER   Shielded from the voices even of his own subjects, the Emperor at Kyoto lives in ignorance of what occurs beyond his palace walls. Normally he would not know about these new barbarian invaders. He would not know about Lord Abe's inability to drive them out. Normally he would not know, and yet—he has been told. By whom? And for what reason?

(TWO LORDS OF THE SOUTH enter and bow before the EMPEROR. The PRIEST picks up the sticks which control the puppet's arms and, through the EMPEROR, acknowledges their bow)

No doubt the presence of these two great Lords of the South will provide us with a clue.

SECOND LORD   With the Emperor's permission.

FIRST LORD   Brought here to amuse His Holiness—the southern provinces' most celebrated storyteller.

PRIEST   The Emperor grants his permission.

RECITER *(As the STORYTELLER enters and kneels before the*

101

EMPEROR) How thoughtful of these Lords to offer a diversion to their Emperor in this time of crisis. But listen carefully, for the tale which they have chosen may well reveal another, more sinister motive for their visit.

STORYTELLER (*Slowly opening a fan*) The Tale of the Courageous King. Across the Straits of Tsushima lies the isolated Kingdom of Korea, a land of peace and harmony. One day, a royal hunting party set out from Seoul in search of tigers near the river bank. While his hunters beat the bush, the young Korean King retired to a sunny glade, and sipped green tea—

(*The fan becomes a cup*)

—prepared by his companion, his Lord High Protector. Around his head buzzed sleepy bees—

(*The closed fan describes a graceful arc around his head*)

—and past him darted brilliant butterflies.

(*The fan is opened and becomes a butterfly*)

Languidly, he raised a single finger and one of the graceful creatures fluttered down upon it.

(*The fan descends and quivers on the* STORYTELLER'*s fingertip*)

"Observe," his Lord Protector smiled, "how even creatures of the field obey your royal summons." Then suddenly the butterfly was gone—for like the King it heard the beaters drawing closer through the bush.

(*The fan floats up, is quickly closed, then slapped down rhythmically in the* STORYTELLER'*s hand to sound like beaters*)

Deep in the forest, the underbrush began to dip and wave—

(*The fan becomes the underbrush*)

—and snapping twigs—

(*Several snaps from the fan*)

—and tearing leaves all heralded the beast's approach! The Lord Protector drew his sword to meet the tiger's rush—

(*The fan becomes the sword*)

—the bamboo trees were thrust aside and there appeared— no tiger, but a man! Then two men, three, then more than one could count. Bearded men with pale white skin, waving swords and spears. "We are emissaries from the King of France, come to open up Korea, come to civilize the savages!" When he heard that, the Lord Protector cast aside his sword and fled. The King was left alone. Oh, what will become of him, abandoned by his treacherous protector? Surely the savages from across the sea will cut him down! But look . . . how superbly he stands his ground! Look how his sword leaps from its scabbard! One Frenchman—gored in the stomach! Another! See how the head flies from the body! And another! Another! Now hear the shouts, hear the roars of defiance as the King's faithful beaters rush to his side. All join in the fray as the screams of the dying Frenchmen echo and reecho down the forest ravine. Oh yes, here was a great victory—for in an hour not a single barbarian was left alive, as once again the butterflies returned to float and shimmer over the wild flowers, dyed crimson by the blood of foreigners. And then, just as the young King sheathed his sword, into the glade strode a magnificent tiger. "Your Majesty," the tiger said, "you are the king of your domain, and I the king of mine. But from the forest I have watched you fight these Western beasts, and surely you, and you alone, deserve to wear the royal crown." So saying, he kow-towed and led the hunters in a shout: "All Hail the King! All Hail our Courageous King!"

(*The* STORYTELLER *bows as the* NOBLES *turn to face the* EMPEROR *and quietly applaud*)

RECITER   An intriguing performance. But one wonders what message the Lords of the South intended to convey. For, unlike the Korean King, the Emperor cannot take up arms and drive the Westerners away. That is the Shogun's duty. Unless, of course, the Shogun—failing in his duty—were forced to step aside.

(*He smiles in mock surprise at his apparent insight*)

ACT II

Scene 4

KAYAMA *and* MANJIRO *kneel at either side of the stage before small, delicate Japanese tables. Both* MEN *wear traditional robes.* KAYAMA *is writing on a small scroll with a brush. Occasionally he dips the brush into a shallow lacquer ink bowl. Beneath his table is a box. Arranged in front of* MANJIRO *is the paraphernalia for the tea ceremony—an earthenware cup, a tea caddy, a bamboo spoon, a bamboo whisk. Next to him is a cast-iron kettle and brazier stand, with a bamboo dipper.* MANJIRO *contemplates these objects silently.*

RECITER   Two men, whose fortunes have been altered by the Westerners' arrival. Manjiro, the common fisherman made samurai. And Kayama Yesaemon, the minor samurai made governor.

(*Reading as* KAYAMA *writes*)

A letter from Kayama Yesaemon to the Shogun. My Lord Abe. It is my privilege to inform you of the current state of our relationship with foreigners here in Uraga.

(KAYAMA *removes a bowler hat from the box under his table and examines it*)

As you have doubtless learned from servants far more worthy than myself, there are now two hundred Westerners among us. Five times as many as a year ago—when they first came.

KAYAMA (*Sings*)
It's called a bowler hat.
I have no wife.
The swallow flying through the sky
Is not as swift as I
Am, flying through my life.
You pour the milk before the tea.
The Dutch ambassador is no fool.
I must remember that.

> (STAGEHANDS *enter and replace* KAYAMA's *writing brush with a steel pen. They add a line or two to his face.* MANJIRO *is similarly aged, but everything else about him remains unchanged. The* RECITER *continues with* KAYAMA's *letter*)

RECITER Three years ago we set aside one district of the town for Westerners, and yet we are still unable to provide them with residences which they consider suitable. For this I humbly ask your indulgence.

KAYAMA
I wear a bowler hat.
They send me wine.
The house is far too grand.
I've bought a new umbrella stand.
Today I visited the church beside the shrine.
I'm learning English from a book.
Most exciting.
It's called a bowler hat.

> (STAGEHANDS *add a touch of gray to* KAYAMA's *and* MANJIRO's *hair.* MANJIRO *begins the tea ceremony. Meanwhile* KAYAMA's *table is replaced by a more Western*

one. He is given a chair. During all this the RECITER
reads)

RECITER   Of all the Westerners with whom I have to deal, the
merchants are most worrisome. They import goods we do
not need, and export those we cannot do without. Last
month they bought and shipped to Shanghai so much flour
that the price here almost tripled. The noodlemakers were
affected most severely and threatened to set fire to the Western warehouses. I found it necessary to restrain them.

(KAYAMA *takes a watch from his pocket*)

KAYAMA
It's called a pocket watch.
I have a wife.
No eagle flies against the sky
As eagerly as I
Have flown against my life.
One smokes American cigars.
The Dutch ambassador was most rude.
I will remember that.

(*As* MANJIRO *continues the tea ceremony,* STAGEHANDS
place a nineteenth-century tea service on KAYAMA's
*table, and pour him a cup of tea which he sweetens and
lightens*)

RECITER   Although the Westerners have been in residence for
upwards of six years now, our samurai still mistake their foreign manners for disrespect. To avoid unpleasant incidents,
I have required all samurai to remove their swords before
entering the city.

KAYAMA
I wind my pocket watch.

We serve white wine.
The house is far too small.
I killed a spider on the wall.
One of the servants thought it was a lucky sign.
I read Spinoza every day.
Formidable.
Where is my bowler hat?

> (STAGEHANDS *replace* KAYAMA's *table with a desk and revolving chair. The hat is removed.* MANJIRO *sips from his cup three times, rests, then finishes it*)

RECITER   I will not bother you with details of the rowdy sailors and adventurers who plague our port. As you know, provisions of the treaties which you signed eight years ago make it impossible for me to deal with them. But fortunately, the behavior of the foreign consuls and ambassadors themselves has been above reproach. They have built themselves a club, complete with bar and billiard room. And only gentlemen may enter.

> (KAYAMA *slowly spins around in his chair; he sports a monocle*)

KAYAMA
It's called a monocle.
I've left my wife.
No bird exploring in the sky
Explores as well as I
The corners of my life.
One must keep moving with the times.
The Dutch ambassador is a fool.
He wears a bowler hat.

> (MANJIRO *finishes the ceremony, rises and dresses him-*

self for sword practice. A French oil painting is hung on the screen behind KAYAMA)

RECITER   My lord, here in Uraga we have reached an understanding with the Westerners. Of course I wish them gone, but I shall try to turn their presence into an advantage rather than a burden. Last week I joined them in a fox hunt.

(KAYAMA *puts on glasses*)

KAYAMA
They call them spectacles.
I drink much wine.
I take imported pills.
I have a house up in the hills
I've hired British architects to redesign.
One must accommodate the times
As one lives them.
One must remember that.

RECITER   Your humble servant, Kayama Yesaemon.

(A STAGEHAND *runs on with a gray tailcoat, and holds it out to* KAYAMA)

KAYAMA
It's called a cutaway . . .

(*He exits, followed by the* STAGEHAND; *a beat, then* MANJIRO *exits, completely dressed*)

ACT II

Scene 5

An empty stage.

RECITER   Ten years ago, Mr. Jonathan Goble visited Japan as a marine aboard one of Perry's ships. Now he has returned, to bring us an American invention which he claims will revolutionize all forms of city transport in Japan. Mr. Goble!

(*The* RECITER *dons a Stetson hat and walks to Center Stage, where he is joined by a ricksha pulled on by a frail* OLD MAN; *to the audience*)

It's my own original design, y'understand. I had one made up special when my wife took sick and couldn't get around. Last month I had it tested in Chicago.

(*A fat, affluent Japanese* MERCHANT *enters*)

A beauty, ain't she?

MERCHANT   Interesting. How does it work?

RECITER/GOBLE   Climb in, my friend. Have a seat. I'll demonstrate. Chop, chop.

(*The* RECITER *and the* MERCHANT *take seats in the ricksha. The* OLD MAN *who pulled it on picks up the poles and begins running in place*)

As ya can see, the ride is smooth and comfortable. Just put your feet up and enjoy the breeze!

(*He offers the* MERCHANT *a cigar*)

Stogie?

MERCHANT   No thank you.

(*The* OLD MAN *begins to show the wear and tear*)

RECITER/GOBLE   She really moves, don't she? Turns in very little space.Great advantage in the crowded streets of Yoko-
hama.

(*The* OLD MAN *is panting now*)

The motor's self-contained, requires very little mainte-
nance—

(*The* OLD MAN *collapses*)

—and can be easily replaced.

(TWO STAGEHANDS *pick the* OLD MAN *up and carry him
to the side. Meanwhile, a* SECOND OLD MAN *takes his
place and continues to run in place. The* STAGEHANDS
revive the FIRST OLD MAN *and stand him up*)

MERCHANT   A remarkable invention. How did you hit upon
it?

RECITER/GOBLE   Modeled it on our Western baby carriage, although in the United States they're pushed instead of
pulled.

MERCHANT   Extraordinary. I don't suppose you'd need a local
merchant's help?

(*The* SECOND OLD MAN *collapses. The* STAGEHANDS *drag
him out of the way and revive him while a* THIRD OLD
MAN *takes his place*)

RECITER/GOBLE   I might. Before I can begin to turn 'em out, there are three things that I'm gonna need. Workin' capital. Workin' capital to purchase raw materials.

MERCHANT   That can be easily arranged.

RECITER/GOBLE   A manufacturin' permit, issued by the government.

(*The* THIRD OLD MAN *collapses and is pulled over to the side to be revived*)

MERCHANT   A simple matter of distributing the proper filing fees.

(*A* FOURTH OLD MAN *enters and painfully tries to lift the poles of the ricksha*)

RECITER/GOBLE   And a supply of laborers who'll work efficiently, and do what they are told.

MERCHANT   Don't be concerned. That is never a problem here.

RECITER/GOBLE (*Enthusiastically*)   My friend, you got yourself a partner! We gonna git ourselves a factory—

(*The* FOURTH OLD MAN *collapses*)

—mebbe two. We gonna turn these beauties out dirt cheap, and sell 'em all across Japan. Why, before you know it—

(*A* FIFTH OLD MAN *enters as the* RECITER *steps down. The* FIFTH OLD MAN *starts to pull the ricksha off*)

—why, before you know it—

(*To the audience, dropping* GOBLE's *persona*)

—before you know it, every city in our country will be overrun by rickshas. Invented, manufactured, marketed by Westerners—

> (*He looks at the line of* OLD MEN, *then hurls away his Stetson hat*)

—but pulled by Japanese.

> (*The* OLD MEN *collapse*)

ACT II

Scene 6

MANJIRO *enters, followed by an* OLDER SAMURAI. *The* TWO MEN *are fencing,* MANJIRO *taking a lesson from the* OLDER MAN. *A beautiful* GIRL *enters behind them, carrying tea things on a small low table.*

GIRL   Father.

OLDER SWORDSMAN   Manjiro has not yet finished with his exercises. Leave the table there.

(*The* GIRL *puts the table down, bows, and crosses Upstage to an imaginary garden, intermittently dipping to the floor and pulling out from her kimono sleeve an azalea. The effect is almost that of a dance. Downstage, the* SWORDSMEN *resume their fencing, silently this time —in mime*)

RECITER   The ancient art of kenjutsu, still practiced by the faithful samurai who have not yet had their heads turned by the wonders of the West.

(*He follows the fencing for a moment, emitting an occasional shout or grunt for the silent* SWORDSMEN.

Upstage of the GIRL, *a* STAGEHAND *enters and places a small wall, 2' high and 3' long. Gracefully, delicately, she continues plucking flowers from her sleeve while the* SWORDSMEN *fence. Upstage of the wall,* THREE BRITISH SAILORS *enter*)

114

FIRST SAILOR   'Ello, look at this.

SECOND SAILOR   That's a lovely piece of work.

FIRST SAILOR   D'ya suppose she's one of those geisha girls?

THIRD SAILOR   'Ere, we'll soon find out. Give us a leg up.

(*Wooden blocks are beaten at the side of the stage, and the* SWORDSMEN *disappear Downstage Left, reappearing Upstage Left and crossing Right.*

The SAILORS *disappear Upstage Right, reappear Downstage and enter Left.*

A STAGEHAND *places the wall Downstage; another, the tea table Upstage. In other words, Upstage Right becomes Downstage Right.*

The wood blocks stop)

FIRST SAILOR   'Ello, look at this.

SECOND SAILOR   That's a lovely piece of work.

FIRST SAILOR   D'ya suppose she's one of those geisha girls?

THIRD SAILOR   'Ere, we'll soon find out. Give us a leg up.

(*He vaults the fence and then helps the* OTHERS *over. He crosses to the* GIRL)

Don't be afraid. We don't mean you any 'arm. 'Arry's my name and these two are my mates.

(*The* TWO SAILORS *tip their hats and smile*)

What pretty flowers. D'ya suppose that I could 'ave one?

(*She gives him one*)

Thank you. That's lovely.

FIRST SAILOR   'Ere. And one for his mates?

THIRD SAILOR   There's a nice lady.

SECOND SAILOR   Much obliged.

THIRD SAILOR   (*Sings*)
  Pretty lady in the pretty garden, cantcher stay?
  Pretty lady, we got leave and we got paid today.
  Pretty lady with the flower,
  Give a lonely sailor 'alf an hour.
  Pretty lady, can you understand a word I say?
  Don't go away.

FIRST SAILOR (*Sings*)
  Pretty lady, you're the cleanest thing I seen all year.

THIRD SAILOR (*Sings*)
  I sailed the world for you.

FIRST SAILOR
  Pretty lady, you're enough to make me glad I'm here.

    (*Simultaneously*)

SECOND SAILOR
  Pretty lady, could I hear you laugh,
  I ain't heard a lady laugh for I don't know how long.
  I'll sing a song for you,
  Tell you tales of adventuring, strange and fantastical.
  Pretty lady, I ain't never been away from home.
  Pretty lady, beg your pardon,
  Wontcher walk me through your pretty garden?

THIRD SAILOR
  Pretty lady, I'm a million miles from Stepney Green.
  You are the softest thing I ever seen.

Stay with me please, I been away so long.
Don't be afraid . . . hey . . .
No, listen, pretty lady, beg your pardon,
Wontcher walk me through your pretty garden?

FIRST SAILOR
Pretty lady, how about it?
Dontcher know how long I been without it?
Pretty lady in the garden, wotcher say?
Cantcher stay? . . . Hey, wait, don't go yet.
Pretty lady with the pretty bow,
Please don't go, it's early.
Wontcher walk me through your pretty garden?

ALL SAILORS
Pretty lady, look I'm on my knees,
Pretty please.

FIRST SAILOR (*Speaks*)   What do we do now?

THIRD SAILOR   I think we're supposed to offer money.

  (*Holding all his money out to her*)

'Ere, is this enough?

  (*She cowers*)

No? Come on blokes, cough it up. 'Ow's this? Is this enough?

  (*They are surrounding her*)

'Tsall we've got. Please?

SECOND SAILOR   (*Sings*)
Pretty lady in the pretty garden, wontcher stay?

FIRST AND THIRD SAILORS
Pretty lady, we got leave and we got paid today.

FIRST SAILOR
  Pretty lady with the flower . . .

ALL
  Give a lonely sailor 'alf an hour.

FIRST SAILOR
  Pretty lady in the pretty garden, wontcher stay?

SECOND SAILOR
  Pretty lady in the pretty garden, wontcher stay?

THIRD SAILOR
  Pretty lady in the pretty garden, wotcher say?

FIRST SAILOR
  Why can't you stay?

SECOND SAILOR
  I sailed the world for you . . .

THIRD SAILOR
  Don't go away . . .

GIRL (*Calls in alarm*)   Father!

OLDER SWORDSMAN (*Standing and turning*)   What is this?

THIRD SAILOR   Pardon me, sir. 'Arry's the name. I'm afraid
  there's been a—

> (*The* OLDER SWORDSMAN *cuts the* THIRD SAILOR *down.
> The* OTHERS *run, but the* FIRST SAILOR *is slashed by the*
> SWORDSMAN *as he scrambles back over the wall.*
>
> STAGEHANDS *enter and clear the stage*)

ACT II

Scene 7

A SAMURAI BODYGUARD *enters, followed by two palanquins, each one carried by* TWO BEARERS. *Inside are* KAYAMA *and* LORD ABE. *Their journey is described by screens which follow their progress.*

RECITER The Tokaido, the royal road from Edo to Kyoto. Kayama Yesaemon reports to Lord Abe on the murder of the English sailor.

ABE You are sure that the indemnity was properly delivered?

KAYAMA My lord, I gave it to the English Ambassador myself.

ABE And he was satisfied?

KAYAMA With the money, yes my lord. But he insisted that he receive the Emperor's apology to Queen Victoria in three days' time.

ABE He shall. We will have the Emperor seal the letter of apology tonight, then send it back to Edo by our fastest runners. What about the samurai who cut the sailors down?

KAYAMA They have been reprimanded, my lord. But it seemed unwise to punish them. Certain Lords, the Lords of the South, are treating them as heroes, calling them the true defenders of Japan.

(ABE *snorts*)

There is a phrase, my lord. A slogan that they have adopted. "Restore the Emperor and Expel the Barbarians."

ABE (*Bitterly*) Any fool can argue that the Westerners should be expelled. Expelling them is something else again.

(*Pause*)

What do these Lords propose? That we attack the English cannon with our swords? That we sink the Russian steamships with our pikes? There is only one way. We must appease the Westerners until we have learned the secrets of their power and success. Then, when we have become their equals. Then, perhaps. Then, if we are sure the time is right—

(A STAGEHAND *enters and indicates falling rain with a fluttering fan; to the* BEARERS)

You there, close up these palanquins before we are soaked through to the skin.

(*The procession pauses while the palanquins are closed. Suddenly* FOUR ASSASSINS *appear from behind the screens*)

ABE What is it?

(*The* BEARERS *run as the* ASSASSINS *attack. As the fight rages,* ABE *is killed in his palanquin. Finally the* SAMURAI BODYGUARD *kills the last* ASSASSIN. *He then crosses to* ABE's *body and examines it*)

KAYAMA (*Sheathing his sword*) These were no ordinary bandits. They were assassins.

SAMURAI Look at the crests beneath their cloaks and you will see who sent them.

KAYAMA   The Lords of the South!

SAMURAI   "Restore the Emperor."

(*A* CLOAKED FIGURE, *who has remained in the back-ground, now steps forward*)

CLOAKED FIGURE (*Completing the* SAMURAI'S *phrase*)   "Expel the Barbarians."

(*The* CLOAKED FIGURE *and the* SAMURAI *fight, and the* SAMURAI *is killed. The* CLOAKED FIGURE *then removes his wraps and reveals himself as* MANJIRO)

KAYAMA   Manjiro! You—one of them? You, who were the first to welcome the Americans.

MANJIRO   What was I then? An ignorant country boy, less than an animal. What am I now? Will you draw your sword as a fellow samurai or shall I cut you down like the Western dog you have become?

KAYAMA   I should have known! Conspirator—murderer—fisherman!

(*They fight.* KAYAMA *is killed. The* TWO NOBLES *enter at the rear of the hanamichi carrying the* EMPEROR—*a larger, older version of the puppet from earlier scenes. The* NOBLES *put the puppet/*EMPEROR *down at Center Stage, then bow as the* LORDS OF THE SOUTH *follow them down the hanamichi*)

FIRST LORD   We are greatly pleased, Manjiro. The Emperor will not forget his debt to you.

SECOND LORD   With the Shogun dead, Japan will be Japan again.

(The LORDS kneel on either side of the EMPEROR and pick up the sticks which manipulate his arms)

FIRST LORD   We will kill the Western merchants.

SECOND LORD   We will burn their embassies!

FIRST LORD   In the name of the Emperor we will drive them back into the sea.

LORDS   In the name of the Emperor—

(The LORDS are suddenly interrupted by a voice from the puppet/EMPEROR)

EMPEROR'S VOICE   In the name of the Emperor—enough!

(Long pause as they stare at the puppet. Magically, real hands emerge from the sleeves, break off the puppet sticks, and toss them away. Then the hands strip away the mask, revealing the face of the RECITER. As he continues speaking, STAGEHANDS enter and remove layer upon layer of his imperial robes)

RECITER/EMPEROR   The day when others speak for me is past. From now on, my word shall be law. And mine alone. I am the Emperor Meiji. Rise—and listen! No more will we draw sword, one Japanese against another. Those who have committed murder in my name have been misguided. In the future they will be restrained—along with those who have encouraged them. Rise!

(The NOBLES, the LORDS OF THE SOUTH—everyone on stage begins to rise slowly and listen)

From this day forth, all samurai will put aside their swords and cease to wear their crested robes.

(STAGEHANDS remove MANJIRO's swords and robes. They sever his samurai's topknot with a knife)

They will take up useful trades. Rise!

> (*The* RECITER/EMPEROR's *final layer of robes is removed. Beneath it he wears the gold braid and buttons of a nineteenth-century Western general. He turns to the audience. Pause*)

Yes.

> (*Pause*)

In the name of progress we will turn our backs on ancient ways. We will cast aside our feudal forms, eliminate all obstacles which hinder our development.

> (*Music begins as the stage is cleared, leaving the* RECITER/EMPEROR *alone with a* CHORUS *of* THREE)

We will organize an army and a navy, equipped with the most modern weapons. And when the time is right, we will send forth expeditions to visit with our less enlightened neighbors. We will open up Formosa, Korea, Manchuria and China. We will do for the rest of Asia what America has done for us!

CHORUS
> Streams are flowing.
> See what's coming
> Next!

RECITER/EMPEROR   We will build railroads, foundries, telegraphs and steamships.

CHORUS
> Winds are blowing.
> See what's coming,
> See what's going
> Next!

RECITER/EMPEROR Factories will spring up all across our land.

CHORUS
Roads are turning,
Journey with them.
A little learning—
Next!

RECITER/EMPEROR Foreign architects will reconstruct our cities.

(*The* CHORUS *exits and is replaced by* THREE CONTEM-PORARY JAPANESE BUSINESSMEN)

BUSINESSMEN
Waters churning,
Lightning flashes.
Kings are burning,
Sift the ashes . . .
Next!

RECITER/EMPEROR The day will come when the Western powers will be forced to acknowledge us as their undisputed equals.

(*The entire stage begins to fill with* CONTEMPORARY JAPANESE FIGURES, *everything from* WOMEN *in pantsuits to* TEENAGERS *in leather jackets*)

COMPANY
Tower tumbles,
Tower rises—
Next!

RECITER/EMPEROR And all of this will be achieved—sooner than you think!

COMPANY
Tower crumbles,
Man revises.
Motor rumbles,
Civilizes.
More surprises
Next!

Learn the lesson
From the master.
Add the sugar,
Spread the plaster.
Do it nicer,
Do it faster . . .
Next!

RECITER (*Who has stripped off his* EMPEROR'S *uniform, and stands in plain black pants and t-shirt*)
The practical bird,
Having no tree of its own,
Borrows another's.

COMPANY
Streams are roaring,
Overspilling—
Next!
Old is boring,
New is thrilling,
Keep exploring—
Next!
First the thunder—
Just a murmur—
A little blunder—
Next!

Then the wonder—
See how pretty!
(Going under—
What a pity!)
Next!
Streams are flying,
Use the motion—
Next!
Streams are drying—
Mix a potion.
Streams are dying—
Try the ocean.
Brilliant notion—
Next!

Never mind a small disaster.
Who's the stronger, who's the faster?
Let the pupil show the master—
Next!
Next!

A VOICE   There are 223 Japan Airlines ticket offices in 153 cities throughout the world.

COMPANY
Next!

ANOTHER VOICE   There are 8 Toyota dealerships in the city of Detroit, and Seiko watch is the third best selling watch in Switzerland.

COMPANY
Next!

THIRD VOICE   Fifty-seven percent of the Bicentennial souvenirs sold in Washington, D.C. in 1975 were made in Japan.

COMPANY
  Next!

FOURTH VOICE   This year Japan will export 16 million kilo-
  grams monosodium glutamate, and 400,000 tons polyvinyl
  chloride resin.

COMPANY
  Next!

FIFTH VOICE   From the Ministry of Health: by 1978 some of
  the beaches on the Inland Sea will be reopened for public
  bathing.

COMPANY
  Next!

SIXTH VOICE   1975 Weather Bureau statistics report 162 days
  on which the air quality in Tokyo was acceptable.

COMPANY
  Next!

  Never mind a small disaster!
  Who's the stronger, who's the faster?
  Let the pupil show the master
  Next!
  Next!
  Next!
  Next!

      (*There is a frenzied dance, suddenly interrupted by the*
      RECITER)

RECITER   Nippon. The Floating Kingdom.

      (*Wood blocks usher on the traditionally dressed figures
      of* KAYAMA *and* TAMATE, *who pass silently through the*
      COMPANY)

There was a time when foreigners were not welcome here.
But that was long ago. One hundred and twenty years.

(*Pause*)

Welcome to Japan.

COMPANY   (*Singing*)
Next! Next!
Brilliant notions,
Still improving—
Next! Next!
Make the motions,
Keep it moving—
Next!
Next!
Next!
Next!

BLACKOUT

Pacific Overtures

**Music and lyrics by Stephen Sondheim
Book by John Weidman
Additional material by Hugh Wheeler
Originally produced and directed
on Broadway by Harold Prince**

*Illustrated with a drawing by Al Hirschfeld
and photographs*

In both its style and subject matter, *Pacific Overtures* is unique in the history of the American musical theater. It tells the story of Commodore Matthew Perry's 1853 expedition to Japan, and describes the upheaval which resulted when America's gunboat diplomacy forced the Japanese to forsake their self-imposed policy of national isolation. It is a play concerned with "progress," and both explicitly and implicitly it raises universal questions about tradition, change, and the cost of modernization.

The style of *Pacific Overtures* reflects and reinforces its thematic concerns in an unprecedented way. A musical play in the great tradition of American musicals, *Overtures* nonetheless incorporates the dramatic techniques of the Japanese kabuki theater. Eastern devices are freely adapted and fused with western stage techniques to produce a theatrical experience both as familiar and exotic as a stroll down Tokyo's eastern/western Ginza. *Pacific Overtures* is a musical unlike any other. It demands to be seen—and read.